CARING FOR THE SOUL

CARING FOR THE SOUL

The Journey to a Healthier and Happier Life

PETER M. KALELLIS

Paulist Press
New York / Mahwah, NJ

The Scripture quotations contained herein are from the New Revised Standard Version: Catholic Edition, Copyright © 1989 and 1993, by the Division of Christian Education of the National Council of the Churches of Christ in the United States of America. Used by permission. All rights reserved.

Cover image by Boule/Shutterstock.com
Cover design by Kate Mayr
Book design by Lynn Else

Copyright © 2020 by Peter M. Kalellis

All rights reserved. No part of this publication may be reproduced, stored in a retrieval system, or transmitted in any form or by any means, electronic, mechanical, photocopying, recording, scanning, or otherwise, without either the prior written permission of the Publisher, or authorization through payment of the appropriate per-copy fee to the Copyright Clearance Center, Inc., www.copyright.com. Requests to the Publisher for permission should be addressed to the Permissions Department, Paulist Press, permissions@paulistpress.com.

Library of Congress Cataloging-in-Publication Data
Names: Kalellis, Peter M., author.
Title: Caring for the soul : the journey to a healthier and happier life / Peter M Kalellis.
Description: New York : Paulist Press, 2020.
Identifiers: LCCN 2019004840 (print) | LCCN 2019981137 (ebook) | ISBN 9780809154838 (pbk. : alk. paper) | ISBN 9781587688799 (ebook)
Subjects: LCSH: Soul—Christianity. | Spiritual life—Christianity. | Spirituality—Christianity.
Classification: LCC BT741.3 .K35 2019 (print) | LCC BT741.3 (ebook) | DDC 233/.5—dc23
LC record available at https://lccn.loc.gov/2019004840
LC ebook record available at https://lccn.loc.gov/2019981137

ISBN 978-0-8091-5483-8 (paperback)
ISBN 978-1-58768-879-9 (e-book)

Published by Paulist Press
997 Macarthur Boulevard
Mahwah, New Jersey 07430
www.paulistpress.com

Printed and bound in the
United States of America

A Prayer for the Beginning of the Day

*Grant me, Lord,
To greet the coming day in peace.
Help me in all things to rely upon Your Holy will.
In every hour of the day, reveal Your will to me.
Bless my dealings with all who surround me.
Teach me to treat all that comes to me throughout the day
with the firm conviction that Your will governs all.
In all my deeds and words,
guide my thoughts and feelings.
In unforeseen events, let me not forget
that all are sent by You.
Enable me to act firmly and wisely,
without embittering or embarrassing others.
Give me strength to bear the fatigue of this day
with all that it shall bring.
Direct my will;
teach me to pray;
pray Yourself in me. Amen.*

—St. Philaret (1867)

CONTENTS

Acknowledgments ix
Introduction xi
  1. What Is the Soul? 1
  2. Your Immortal Self 7
  3. Our Inner Journey 15
  4. The Power of the Soul 21
  5. Listening to the Soul 27
  6. Finding Peace 33
  7. The Pursuit of Peace 39
  8. Caring for Your Soul 45
  9. The Quest for Happiness 53
10. The Quest for Joy 59
11. The Fear of Death 69
12. Dealing with Grief 77
13. Pruning and Maturing 83
14. You Will Never Die! 87
Epilogue 95

ACKNOWLEDGMENTS

Writing this book has been a rewarding experience, not only because it has helped me to reflect on the invaluable gifts of life and love, but also because the process of writing involves a community of people who continually support me on this journey.

I am indebted to the support of my dear wife, Pat, who sustains me through the difficult moments in the writing process and is also my most trusted critic.

I am also grateful for my children and grandchildren, who continue to encourage me and give me joy in life.

Of course, I am most grateful for the ongoing support of Fr. Mark-David Janus, publisher at Paulist Press, and his editorial, production, and marketing teams: in particular, Trace Murphy and Donna Crilly in the editorial department; Diane Flynn and Kimberly Bernard in production; Lynn Else in design; and Bob Byrns and Gloria Capik in marketing. I am also thankful to my editor, Paul McMahon, who always provides valuable input on the editing process. All these people help to make the book a reality and get it into the hands of the reader.

Finally, I am most grateful for the gift of faith in a God who gives me hope and has constantly taught me the way to care for my soul throughout my life. It is an ongoing lifetime lesson.

INTRODUCTION

I'm sure you have been told repeatedly what you must do to be physically healthy. Exercising daily by taking a brisk walk or a half-hour swim is a good minimum exercise. Eating three light and nutritious meals daily will provide energy and can maintain a healthy weight range. Take one multivitamin tablet every day and supplemental minerals as needed, especially folic acid, B12, and B6. Have a complete physical examination at least once a year. A good night's sleep is also very important. Without enough sleep, the quality of what you do will decrease; rising early requires going to bed at a reasonable hour. Avoid smoking and drugs that are supposed to make you feel high. Consume alcohol in moderation. A good massage once every four to six weeks can revitalize and relax your body. Enjoy experiences in nature: visiting a park, hiking, walking, playing tennis, and so on.

When you face emotional problems, boredom, conflicts, anger, depressive or negative feelings, a sense of emptiness, or lack of direction, professionals in the healing arts—psychologists, psychiatrists, psychotherapists, and marriage and family therapists—can be helpful. To a large degree, the above guidelines provide the foundation for a healthy body and a sound mind, and you realize how important they are for a healthier and happier life of inner contentment and joyful and peaceful physical existence. But there is another important question.

Where do we get the energy to practice these guidelines? This mysterious power that keeps our bodies and minds functioning and keeps us alive is our soul, or spirit. Each day, you meet your physical needs—eating, resting, sleeping at regular intervals, and making efforts to keep your body in good health. How do we make time for spiritual renewal? If we neglect our bodies, they become weak and break down. If we neglect our spiritual needs, we become emotionally confused and conflicts upset our daily rhythm.

When your emotional vision becomes blurred, it is time to close your eyes and reflect and search deeper for the force that nurtures your spiritual life. This book is not a practical manual. The reader does not have to create an imaginary soul, a psyche. The psyche is already there. It has kept you alive thus far, and it will keep you alive for the rest of your earthly life. But if it is currently tormenting you, you need to know what mysterious factors are alienating you or blocking your peace. If you feel trapped in the struggle for prestige, recognition, and appearances, you are probably a victim of wishful thinking. Concepts of what should be, what ought to be, or how society, government, and the world should be are mind mechanisms that lead to fantasy.

During the last fifty years, psychotherapy, a tedious and expensive road to self-recovery, has branched out and blossomed in our society, promising solutions to lifelong problems. Many people have benefited from therapy of one sort or another. In recent years, many professionals in the healing arts have tried to explore a deeper part of our humanity, the

Introduction

spiritual self. They discovered that most emotional problems are a result of an ailing soul.

The following chapters will give you a better understanding of the inner part of your being—your spiritual self, your soul—which maintains your physical existence. And then, you and I may have to face our unique challenge: If we do so much for our physical self, our body, how can we take care of our soul?

1

WHAT IS THE SOUL?

When we ask, what is the soul? *it is like asking,* what is God? *Does anyone know? To attain any assured knowledge about the soul is one of the most difficult things for the human mind. Science, by engaging the mind, logic, and reason, explores and defines whatever is tangible with sufficient accuracy. However, unseen realities— God, the soul, the spirit—require faith, assisted by prayer and meditation.*

Do you ever wonder, *What is the soul?* Most people do, and we don't really have easy answers because the soul is a spiritual power that keeps us alive. Rational thinking tells us that a light bulb without electricity cannot give light. A space suit without an astronaut is just a space suit. A brand new expensive car without an engine is useless. A body without a soul is dead.

Our wish to understand, even partially, the essence and properties of the soul requires spiritual resources. It can only be done in the human heart, not in a scientific laboratory.

Progressive knowledge about the soul contributes to our understanding of ourselves, God, and the world around us. Although the soul abides in the body, it is not located in any specific part of the body. And yet, there is no functional part of the body in which the soul is not wholly present. In all major religions, God acts in nature and governs the universe; in like manner, the soul moves and activates each member of the body to perform its function. It permeates the entire body, giving it life. In other words, the soul is not enclosed by the body but occupies the body to which it is attached. The soul is not held by the body. The soul gives the body life.

The soul's faculty is expressed in the universal yearning for God. It is life, God's gift to humans, and it is ever connected with its Creator. Nothing in the created world can satisfy the soul. Created by God, the soul seeks and wants to live in communion with God. Until the soul has attained this, it cannot find peace. How much better it would be to move our life daily in the direction of God. It is the soul that responds to every movement by God's grace.

Accepting the concept of such an unexplored potential as relating to God, intrinsic qualities that are good in us can mean the difference between success and failure, love or lack of love, happiness or unhappiness. The heart is the center of the human psychosomatic constitution. There is an unconfused union between soul and body. Therefore, the heart is not only the physical organ that pumps blood through our body, it is the source of all emotions; it has the abundant capacity for spiritual feelings such as compassion, faith, hope, peace, and love. This capacity indicates that we are not only physical entities, we are also spiritual beings.

What Is the Soul?

Like the conductor of an orchestra, the soul harmonizes our patterns and inner qualities to give us a fuller sense of who we are and a better appreciation of our earthly purpose. This activity releases the divine energy within, restores our daily life, and brings us closer to our Creator. Although invisible to the human eye, our soul is the divine part of our humanity, which needs to be cared for and nurtured.

How do you relate to your soul? How is your relationship with your inner self? When was the last time you stopped your busy activity (of caring for cars, clothes, fulfilling desires, of having fun, and other things) and thought about your soul?

Many believe that conflicts and emotional problems relate to the way we grew up, our way of perceiving and interacting with others, but have nothing to do with our spiritual self. Yet it is obvious that our inner self, the soul, the seat of our deepest emotions, can benefit greatly from the gifts of an active spiritual life. We miss the joy of life when the soul is deprived spiritually. Religions around the world promote that the spiritual life requires constant attention, but it is easier to become lodged in the material world and forget the spiritual realm. Sacred technology is aimed largely at helping us to remain conscious of spiritual ideas and values. We are showered with information about living healthily, but we have largely lost the sense of our body's wisdom. If an emotional problem presents itself, the real issue may not be some single trauma or troubled relationship; the issue is a life where the soul is neglected. Problems are part of human existence, and they do not necessarily wither the soul. The soul suffers more from the everyday conditions of life when we do not nourish it with the solid experiences it craves.

FOR FURTHER CONSIDERATION

✦ If we are to consider caring for the soul, and if we believe that the soul is nurtured in an environment of beauty, then we need to understand beauty more deeply and give it a more prominent place in our life. As you enter an old Orthodox church, you can be suddenly confronted with unimaginable beauty—the beauty of its structure, the greatness of the screen that separates the altar from the church attendants, and the Byzantine iconography—and as you hear the chanting, you are transformed for a few moments. Your soul is in utter ecstasy.

✦ Most religions have always understood the value of beauty, as is evident in their churches and temples, which are never built for purely practical considerations. Through the imagination these buildings evoke feelings of respect and gratitude.

✦ Similarly, a huge belfry, steeple, or stained glass window is not purely for a practical purpose. Each speaks to the soul's need for beauty, for love of the building itself, and for sacred imagination and individual inspiration.

✦ We can learn from our churches or temples, and attend to this same need in our homes, our commercial buildings, our workplace, our highways, our schools, and our centers of education.

What Is the Soul?

✦ An appreciation for beauty is an openness to the power of ordinary things to nurture the soul. If we can be affected by beauty, then the soul is alive and well in us. The soul's extraordinary talent is to be affected. Basically, the word *passion* means "to be affected," and passion is the essential energy of the soul.

2

YOUR IMMORTAL SELF

> *Because of the soul's incorporeality [spiritual essence], "the soul's beauty is harder to see...." The soul is concerned with goodness and beauty, with justice and courage, with friendship and loyalty.*
>
> —James Hillman, *The Force of Character*

Human beings have always wondered about life and death, gradually becoming aware of another dimension of their existence—a life force that activates our body and causes us to think that there must be a master builder who created this earth for people to inhabit. We call this part of our human awareness, the soul. The soul searches for its Creator beyond the physical world.

The soul is the unseen part of our body that makes it possible for us to believe that we are God's creation. Just as God rules, sustains, and animates the universe, so does the soul give life to the body. Because the soul is a spiritual being, it does not die. It is immortal. This whole concept existed in pre-Christian times. Ancient Greek philosophers, sages, and wise teachers have always believed that, although the physical body ages and dies, the soul continues to live. In time, these Greek philosophical ideas and practices were adapted and adopted as Christian.

Before we outline some of the Christian concepts of the soul, let us consider what those philosophers, sages, and wise teachers teach about human beings and the soul.

The Stoics taught that all existence was material, and they described the soul as a breath pervading the body. They called it divine—in Greek, *apospasma tou theou*—or more precisely, a particle of God composed of the most refined and ethereal matter, whose seat is the heart, the center of the cognitive and emotional life.

Plato (428–348 BC), in Phaedo's dialogue says,

> The soul is invisible, pure and noble, and on her way to the good and wise God. That soul departs to the invisible world—to the divine and immortal. Upon arriving, she lives in bliss and is released from the error and folly of people, their fears and wild passions and all other human ills, and forever dwells in company of gods.

The immortality of the soul was the principal subject of Plato's speculations. He believed that, upon death, the soul leaves the body and enters a new world, invisible to our physical eyes, and lives forever in the presence of God.

The Neoplatonists supported the dualism of the body, where the soul implies a distinct spirit that is essentially good while the body is evil. Therefore, the body is the "prison," the "tomb," or even the "hell" of the soul—implying that the body is the seat of all sin. Implicit, here, is the thought that as the soul leaves the body, it liberates itself.

Pythagoras (580–500 BC) taught that the soul was harmonious, its essence consisting of those perfect mathematical ratios that are the laws of the universe and the music of the heavenly spheres.

Pythagoras required his followers to lead a harmonious life by practicing virtues: loyalty, resistance to temptations, truthfulness, generosity, honesty, hospitality, and whatever is good and beautiful. Men and women who attended his school in southern Italy were required to practice these spiritual disciplines through self-examination. Pythagoras commanded,

> Do not go to sleep before you examine and question three times your deeds of the day: "What have I trespassed? What good deed have I done? What should I have done but omitted doing?" When you realize that you have done wrong things, reprimand yourself, and if you have done good deeds, rejoice. This you must practice, this you must study, this must be your daily course, because this will put you on the path to divine virtue.

Defined by the Pythagorean school, virtue is order, harmony, and health of the soul. Education should aim to cultivate and establish virtue.

In the Book of Genesis, we learn that God forms Adam's body, and then he breathes into it and creates the soul. The inbreathing of God is the energy of the Holy Spirit. It is this energy that created the soul. The soul cannot be examined apart from its Creator. In Hebrew, three terms are used for the soul: *nephesh*, referring to the animal and vegetative nature; *nuah*, referring to the ethical principle; and *shesamah*, referring to the purely spiritual intelligence. The Old Testament asserts or implies the distinct reality of the soul. In later Jewish thought, Philo of Alexandria teaches with conviction about the divine origin of the soul. But Christianity brings all definitions of the soul to full focus. Tertullian, a Christian of the early church, speaks eloquently of the failure of all philosophies to elucidate the nature of the soul. He points out that only Christ can teach humankind the truth on such a subject. Truly, Christ's teachings center on the spiritual side of human nature:

> You shall love the Lord your God with all your heart, and with all your soul and with all your mind....This is the greatest and first commandment....What shall be the benefit to a man who gains the whole world and loses his soul? What could he give in exchange of his soul?...Be not afraid of those that would kill your body...but rather fear those who can destroy both soul and body.

St. Paul consistently appropriates psyche—the soul—for the natural life. For the supernatural or spiritual life, he uses the term *pheuma*—spirit—which is the Holy Spirit, dwelling and operating in the human heart.

Philosophical and religious thought throughout written history indicates our human realization that we are not simply flesh, bones, and blood. We consist of a physical body and an inner force that animates the body. In most religions, the inner force is known as the soul. Both body and soul coexist simultaneously without any confusion. We are aware that we are more than mere physical entities. There is another part in us that is unseen, yet ever present in our lives.

The human soul is multifaceted. It may be considered as trinitarian in nature: the Greek words *nous*, *logos*, and *pneuma* have their own special connotation—*nous* is the thinking part and core of human existence; the *logos* is the expression of thought and perception of the *nous*; and *pneuma*, the spirit, is the vivifying force of human life.

Paul's hope, the hope that God gave to us in his Word, has only one name: resurrection. Sometime between now and the resurrection, some of us, perhaps all (depending on when the Lord will come—a time nobody knows), will die. St. Paul states confidently,

> We do not want you to be uninformed, brothers and sisters, about those who have died, so that you may not grieve as others do who have no hope. For since we believe that Jesus died and rose again, even so, through Jesus, God will bring with him those who have died. For this we declare to you by the word of the Lord, that we who are alive, who are left until the coming of the Lord, will by no means precede those who have died. For the Lord himself, with a cry of command, with the archangel's call and with the sound of God's trumpet, will descend from heaven, and the dead in Christ will rise first. (1 Thess 4:13–16)

In a time of prayer or meditation, as we get deeper into our self, we become more aware of the unseen attributes of the soul:

The **conscience** is an inner voice that guides us through life's choices and decisions. It is a part of our being that praises what is good and beneficial and judges or even reprimands what is evil and destructive. It is our innate inward call to become part of the Body of Christ. The perfection of conscience is *agape*—love.

The **mind**, *nous*—the highest human faculty—is the ability to think and reason, which precipitates emotions, actions, movements, and survival skills. It is a part of our being that conceives ideas and pursues or avoids their fulfillment. When it is purified, the mind perceives God and his creation.

The **free will** is a human prerogative to make choices, to discern good and evil. As we harmonize conscience, mind, and heart, we can decide with greater confidence what action is proper. We have the freedom to pursue good or evil, to create or to destroy, to live a good life or a destructive life, to love and forgive or to hate. Such discernment results in a life of wisdom, which is the perfection of know-how in being a responsible member of society and, eventually, a true member of God's kingdom.

FOR FURTHER CONSIDERATION

✦ Become partakers of the divine nature, your soul. "For this very reason, you must make every effort to support your faith with goodness, and goodness with knowledge" (2 Pet 1:5).

✦ There is an ancient saying that tells us to get deeper into ourself; explore our soul, the spiritual part of us, and learn from our inner self what we must do.

✦ "The ladder that leads to the Kingdom is hidden within you, and is found in your own soul. Dive into yourself, and in your soul you will discover the rungs by which to ascend" (*The Art of Prayer: An Orthodox Anthology*, p. 164).

3

OUR INNER JOURNEY

It's your road and yours alone. Others may walk it with you, but no one can walk it for you.

—Rumi

Allow me to accompany you on this journey, the intention of which is to acquaint ourselves with the presence and purpose of our soul. This inner journey promises a newness of life. Essentially, we will look deeply into our spiritual self, our soul, where a part of the divine abides, and feel the inner peace and joy that come from exploring our inner self and connecting with our soul.

Our soul is what makes us alive and connecting with it is essential. Sometimes, we get carried away on the wings of worries and fears, hopes and dreams, visions of a future yet to come, and a past that is long gone. Consequently, we forget to care for our soul. There is so much courage, intelligence, and potential that lie beyond the boundaries of our worries and fears. Beyond the boundaries of our worst nightmares lie an immense peace and potential for spiritual growth. Our soul is real...beyond imagination or thinking. More accurately, it is *before* imagination and thinking ever take place. The greatest thing is that our true inner self, our soul, cannot be touched or tampered with by the mind. It exists before the mind has emerged, and is there after the mind subsides. It is profoundly and truly unperturbed. Moreover, it is always there for us to experience.

Life is a great blessing to be cherished every moment as we listen carefully to that inner voice—*the soul's silent whisper*. By listening to and trusting that whisper, we are guided through this journey to higher and new opportunities. To know our inner self, our soul, is to learn who God really is, and our purpose in life. Gradually, we become aware of our motivations, our values, our visions, our goals, and our beliefs; not of what we have been told by others, but what we have discovered ourselves. Ultimately, we discover God's cares and plan for each of us.

Knowing your inner self requires introspection and self-awareness. At the same time, the process of discovery never ends—it's a lifelong journey, a daily unfolding. Time and again, Fr. Paul, who has been my spiritual counselor, told me "to go deeper into myself, connect with my soul and start feeling inspired." He advised, "Your soul will nurture your inspiration and spiritual growth. When you face difficult situations, even when you come up with a logical solution, you might stop before acting. Be patient and wait to hear your soul's voice."

There are moments when logic suggests that we should do something, yet our soul is telling us not to take any action. For example: Perhaps you are having an argument with your partner or a good friend. Deep inside, you know you're not right, but somehow you force yourself into winning the argument, simply because you think, *If I give in, this would show*

Our Inner Journey

that I'm a weak person. There may be other reasons that seem important at the time of the argument, but later are no longer important. Your inner self, your soul, was telling you to stop. Trust that silent voice.

Listening to your inner self, your soul, is crucial for your spiritual development. Your self-growth and the success of personal spiritual development are entirely dependent on how well you are aware that you have a soul that keeps you alive. Judging yourself excessively can damage your self-image. Then your soul suffers and uncomfortable symptoms arise.

My daily self-exploration involves asking questions pertinent to my self-image and my soul's presence. For example, there was a time I was focused on how my parents had wounded me, especially my stepmother and some other adults. As a therapist, listening to other people's problems, I realized how they too have experienced hurt by parents, partners, relatives, or friends. Life's hurts may leave scars, but they are not fatal. Eventually, I concluded that people who hurt us were most likely hurt by others. Each one of us, as well as all who went before us, share the human condition and suffer from imperfect love. Our challenge is that, while we may not be able to stop totally the pain of our hurts or wounds, we can attend to our soul's thirst for healing. Furthermore, while we may not be able to regain the love that we missed from significant others, our soul provides perfect love. By listening to our soul, we can move toward accepting a relationship with God, who loves unconditionally. Our inner journey is nothing more than a return to the safety of our faith, the acceptance and gratitude that our soul is also God's presence within each one of us in our present life.

Your true self is the place where your deepest thoughts live. It is what you ultimately think of yourself, how you treat yourself, and what you fear others might see in you. No one can accurately define your personality, except you.

Until recently, most health professionals believed that our true self is something we are always aiming to pursue. It was regarded as the better part of *you* and *me* that resides in our dreams—being the successful businessman or professional woman that we always dreamed we could become one day. These thoughts of improving or gaining something for ourselves were what once defined becoming our true self. These thoughts, however, are not necessarily accurate.

Let's sharpen our focus by asking a couple of questions: Have you ever done something you wish no one could ever find out about? I know that I have, and chances are, you have too. Do you still remember what it was, and why you didn't, and maybe still don't, want anyone to find out about it? Sometimes, we do things and then try to justify our behavior using events and people we see around us. Other times, we do something only to realize how wrong and destructive it was. This is when we can easily hear our inner voice. Our soul is aware but remains silent until an opportune moment, then whispers, "*It's time to change.*" That's our true self, our soul, giving us a message. This is the voice of the soul that, depending on our character, will either encourage us to take even more actions or discourage us as much as possible from doing the wrong thing again. Whether we believe it or not, this is our true self, which, in most cases, is right.

As you rediscover yourself, you will probably remember the times when you could speak or act freely, without any fear regarding the impact your behavior may have. Do you remember how good you felt? And can you trace what has changed since then? While I'm sure you have your reasons for changing over the past years, probably not all the changes

Our Inner Journey

you've gone through were necessary. Fortunately, there is still time to reclaim your true self.

FOR FURTHER CONSIDERATION

Here are a few suggestions to help you rediscover your inner self:

✦ Respect your goals and values. Your soul is your life here on earth and it continues your life beyond the grave.

✦ It is important to stay at peace with your soul. Respect what's important for you in the long term.

✦ Do not become a slave to other situations where people can manipulate you.

✦ Always value others but avoid doing it at the expense of your own goals and values.

✦ If helping another person may jeopardize your own goals and values, take time to reconsider your thoughts, feelings, and behavior.

4

THE POWER OF THE SOUL

Our heart is restless until it rests in you.

—St. Augustine

We each experience a sense of restlessness, an unhappiness or lack of joy. But what can we do about it? If we believe that, besides our physical self, we have a spiritual dimension—a soul that keeps the body alive—then the challenge is how to care for our soul.

While we abide in our physical body, we need to sustain it through proper nutrition. Most people look routinely for two or three meals a day and plenty of refreshing liquids. But there is another part of us, our soul, that needs spiritual food for its sustenance. Without the required daily input of physical and spiritual nutrition, a neglected body and soul suffer. The body cannot live without food and water, and our spiritual self, our soul, will starve from lack of attention. Many physical diseases occur because of a troubled soul.

Recall the story of a woman named Martha who welcomed Jesus into her home. Martha was distracted by many tasks. She was eager to prepare a luscious dinner for Jesus and wanted to satisfy him. Mary, however, sat by the feet of Jesus and listened to his words. Then Martha came near them and said, "Lord, do you not care that my sister has left me to do all the work by myself? Tell her then to help me" (Luke 10:40).

Looking at her with compassion, Jesus said, "Martha, Martha, you are worried and distracted by many things; there is need of only one thing. Mary has chosen the better part, which will not be taken away from her" (Luke 10:41–42). We find in this story the reality of our dual human needs, the physical and the spiritual. Martha can be praised for her hospitality and thoughtfulness in preparing a meal for Jesus. Mary preferred to nourish her soul. Sitting at the feet of Jesus revived the spirit and satisfied the deepest longings of her soul. She chose "the better part," wanting to hear what Jesus had to say.

We all welcome a delicious meal on the table. Food provides our bodies with the energy we need. Nutritionists teach that the best way to construct a diet is to eat small meals throughout the day—as often as every two to three hours—just enough to "take the edge off" and satisfy the hunger and thirst as we burn away calories. In other words, the best way to manage food is to eat just enough to satisfy the hunger and thirst and replenish our physical energy. Obviously, with work and schedules, this is not possible for most people, so a general compromise is to eat three times daily, and exercise enough to burn the calories we consume.

Some diets can be unhealthy. For example, a "feast or famine" approach is unhealthy because it does not provide steady nourishment. Extreme diets might produce immediate and dramatic weight loss but are rarely sustainable, and often

The Power of the Soul

cause problems with organs that are overtaxed by too much and then too little nourishment.

Our innermost being, our soul, hungers and thirsts for spiritual food. Jesus has a menu of spiritual nutrients to nourish the soul. His filling food is accessed by faith. Jesus said to his followers, "I am the bread of life. Whoever comes to me will never be hungry, and whoever believes in me will never be thirsty" (John 6:35).

Faith in Jesus, and applying his teachings in our life, contribute to a healthy heart as we designate a time for regular and consistent prayer. Appropriating a place in your home, wherever you live, and a time each day to offer a prayer nurtures your soul. You will sense the difference in your disposition and feelings, as it becomes a natural part of your life. Your thirsty soul will be quenched, as often as you drink in the Lord's love, forgiveness, understanding, and wisdom. Feed yourself by faith just as Mary sat by the feet of Jesus and absorbed his words. His grace will feed your heart and soul. Pain and conflict, emotional fatigue and boredom will fade as you turn in faith to the healer of body and soul. By accepting Jesus as your Savior and Redeemer, your life will be enriched, and your thirsty soul will praise his Holy Name. Our Lord Jesus Christ is alive, ready, and willing to fill your hungry heart with faith and satisfy your thirsty soul with contentment and eternal security. Let the ears of your heart hear his loving invitation. "Come to me, all you that are weary and are carrying heavy burdens, and I will give you rest. Take my yoke upon you, and learn from me; for I am gentle and humble in heart, and you will find rest for your souls. For my yoke is easy, and my burden is light" (Matt 11:28–30).

Periodically, I feel gratitude when I recall those innocent years as a seminary student. Fr. Vincent Pottle's advice and counsel were beyond dogma and abstract theological studies. "Feed yourselves with prayer, fasting, scripture study, and charitable actions," he said. "This is the only way to nourish your inner self."

Fr. Pottle must be smiling from above, knowing that some of his students found his advice and counsel beneficial in their lives. For the last four decades, the first thing that I do each morning is to connect in prayer with our Lord, the Giver of my life. My ever-present concern has been how I can better nourish my soul. What few simple words can express my gratitude to the Lord for giving me life for another day?

Some mornings, I must confess, I am either tired or moody and fail to do what is needed. Mornings usually come and go too quickly. I often need to move quickly—get into the bathroom and wash, grab a bite to eat, and run—and sometimes I just don't feel like facing the day. What I really want to do is get back into bed, pull up the covers under my nose, and sleep. Then, in a daze, I ask myself, where am I running? But I have no answer. I need someone, perhaps a wise person, to tell me. Regaining my senses, I realize that what counts most is that somebody may know, and it is my Lord Jesus who understands human nature. Somehow that motivates me. As I get in my car, heading for work, I whisper, "Lord, be with me today. Help me to share with my clients what seems to have helped me this far in my life, and how sharing my experience can prove beneficial to others."

Early in the morning, after I have washed and dressed, I ask the Lord's blessing upon his precious gift of my life. Then I read and meditate on a brief passage from the New Testament. As I read the passage, I close my eyes, take a few deep breaths and try to understand what the Lord is telling me at this moment.

After ten minutes, I offer a prayer for myself, each member of my family, and other people who have asked me to pray for them. This time in prayer usually nourishes and strengthens my inner self. By breakfast time, with rare exceptions, I am in a peaceful, if not happy, state of mind. I also become aware that the things the Lord gives me as food for my soul often become food for other members of my family and for some of my clients in therapy.

What is proper food for our soul? Besides regular prayer, it is reading and meditating on the Word of God. Here again, not the simple reading of the Word of God, so that it only passes through our minds, but meditating on it, considering, pondering, and applying what we read to our lives. When we pray, we speak to God. And to pray for any length of time, we must have at least a small desire to connect with our Creator. The best time to pray is after our inner self has been nourished by meditation on the Word of God, where we find our Lord Jesus speaking to us, comforting us, encouraging us, instructing us, accepting us, and directing us. If you take time for meditation before praying, it will be much easier to stay focused. I emphasize this point because of the great spiritual profit and refreshment I have received from meditation. By applying myself to this practice, God has given me courage and strength to go peacefully through greater trials than I had ever known in my life before.

FOR FURTHER CONSIDERATION

- ✦ Whether you know it or not, your life is a spiritual journey. Every believer is on a spiritual path; it is just a matter of degree. Some pursue it willingly, others do not. In the final analysis, we will all make the grade. It is merely a matter of time and of awareness that God is present each moment of our life.

✦ As for measuring the progress of our journey, its value is not to foster a competitive outlook, but rather to heighten awareness of how we are doing and where we need help to improve our behavior and attitude.

✦ A fundamental tenet of the spiritual life is that existence has a purpose that springs from a Divine Source we call God, and it is not merely a random cosmic accident. Life has very real properties, meaning, and direction. Losing sight of these things does not change the reality of life.

✦ Physical laws govern daily existence; more subtle ones govern our spiritual development. Doubting such laws does not keep them from operating; they simply exist. For instance, an individual slipping from a ladder, regardless of personal beliefs about gravity, will fall. Mental acceptance is irrelevant to that reality.

✦ The world is essentially a school, and life is our schoolwork. All experiences gained through living are multifaceted lessons that serve to educate, entertain, and awaken us spiritually. Just like passing through school, we progress through various life stages. We have lessons, homework, and tests. As we pass our tests, we get new assignments and gradually rise to higher levels of rewarding spiritual life.

5

LISTENING TO THE SOUL

External aspects of life that can occupy our minds may evoke temporary interest, but they create an emptiness within, a sense of shallowness. The less significance we give our thoughts about external issues, the easier it will be for us to connect with our soul, the source of peace and joy.

—Richard Carlson, PhD

Does my soul have a voice? Yes! Deep in your heart, you know what to do and what to avoid, and which of the two is the right direction to take. The voice of the soul may be silent, but its message is of great importance. Like a wise and gentle teacher, this inner voice invites us to follow as it leads us toward a sense of purpose and meaning.

Sit in a quiet, comfortable place where external sounds will not disturb you. Gently place your right hand over your heart and feel the regular beat. You are alive! Ask yourself, "Who or what causes my heart to beat? Who causes my lungs to breathe?

A second question that is of equal importance is, How can I sharpen my hearing so that I can distinguish my own soul's voice from the voices of others? Stay calm and listen. When you are alone in quietness, your soul's voice will speak directly to your mind about issues that you may have to face in your present day. Take three deep breaths, relax for a few seconds, and imagine hearing the voice of your soul. What is it saying to you about your life, family, friends, neighbors, or workplace? Can this inner voice validate who you are, how you respond to your daily encounters with others? And what are your expectations? Are you kind and generous? Are you investing time and energy with others who need your presence? As you interact genuinely with other people, do you discover aspects of your self that need attention?

Most of us hurry through life, filled with drive and ambition in our search for success. We never pause and ask ourselves what happens once we have attained success. Can we hear the voice of our soul that cherishes our success and expresses gratitude in the present, or do other voices prevail, convincing us to pursue more success for our future?

In the 1980s, I wrote the book *Pick Up Your Couch and Walk*. As I was coming to the end of the writing, I wondered what I would do next. Immediately, I decided to write another book and I had already chosen the title, *Five Steps to Spiritual Growth*. Then, as I began to write a prologue for this new title, I started to wonder again what I would be doing when I had completed this book. Again, my answer was to plan the next book.

One day, during a prayerful meditation that took me deeper into my self, the voice of my soul, gentle and clear, informed me that if writing is my passion, enjoy it and be

Listening to the Soul

grateful. However, there is no need to use my passion for writing in search of one success after another.

Success may be attained with intense struggle and may be sweet and pleasant, but it cannot be the destination. Why not? Because it will always seek the next success. Consequently, frustration and negative forces may arise, silencing your soul's voice. And spiritual frustration can sometimes present itself through illness. Disease can be the body's way of telling us that we are not listening to the soul's voice. We can hear this message when we focus on the inner voice of our soul.

Often, when people come to me for therapy, I look for the "disease" within their soul, the suffering physical self. Therapists can never heal anyone. At best, they pave the way to healing, but God is the ultimate healer. On occasion, I might hold up a mirror. If a client chooses to look in the mirror, he or she may begin to speak from the emotional trauma of the past, instead of just from the mind of the present. When this happens, there is the strong possibility that the suffering client may begin to change, growing away from the illness that he or she may have unknowingly created within themselves.

All humans contain the keys to health and wholeness within themselves. When we suffer illness, the medical professionals prescribe different kinds of medicine, hoping to provide healing. But healing ingredients already exist within each human body. Listening to the soul may sometimes take a lifetime, if we choose. The choice is often difficult, for the challenges become greater the less we listen to the voice of our soul.

In our pursuit of spiritual growth, there are many tools available to connect with the soul and hear its voice. Prayer gives us courage and wisdom to access our spiritual life daily.

Prayer comes in many different forms, including meditation. Personally, I have made it my practice to meditate every morning, to center and to reacquaint myself with my soul. To meditate, I sit quietly away from the usual distractions and let thoughts pass through the mind without grabbing onto them, until I get to a place of inner silence and tranquility. Though simple in concept, this is not easy to do. It takes practice and requires tenacity to reach that quiet place and embrace the stillness needed to meet with the soul and hear your inner voice.

FOR FURTHER CONSIDERATION

✦ Let your journey begin. Next time you come against an area of doubt or skepticism, admit to yourself that you have a tough time accepting certain matters that are not tangible. Spiritual realities are difficult to grasp with rational thinking alone. It takes faith and honesty to provide a unique opportunity for peace of mind, helping your perception and spiritual truths.

✦ Doubts do not necessarily mean that you are not a spiritual person. Your confidence is based not on your physical body alone but on the part of yourself that is unseen, your soul.

✦ Your journey is not a race or competition, but rather a means to heighten awareness of how you are doing and where you need help in order to improve your behavior and attitude as well as your awareness that God is present each moment of your life.

✦ Living in a modern world where everything is available to us does not necessarily benefit our well-being. We may be collecting things, trying to keep up with scientific progress, and attaching ourselves to electronic media and technological gadgets. These may become emotional crutches, an illusion of security in an insecure world.

✦ Security cannot be found from outside ourselves, and certainly not behind walls of clutter. Security comes from looking within our spiritual essence and living with faith and integrity. Ultimately, you will hear the soul's voice. Be patient and regain a state of peace in the present.

6

FINDING PEACE

It is difficult to think of our soul or our spiritual life if we don't have peace of mind. It may be hard to pray, to be kind to others, to be loving and charitable if we ourselves are not at peace. Having peace of mind in our life is most important if we want to take care of our soul.

People with good intentions who wish to care for their souls realize that their first step is to be at peace. Worrying about past wrongs or being concerned about what could happen in the future only causes confusion and lack of peace. In caring for our soul, there are ways and thoughts that can help us.

1. *Nothing lasts forever.* Things and situations change. People mature. Friendships and relationships change, evolve, and sometimes fade away. Even when things feel satisfactory, later circumstances may change this. You may have already been through circumstances where you were forced to accept a drastic change and move forward. Even

when that change was particularly difficult, you were able to take steps forward. You pushed through and survived. Your soul, your inner strength, helped you to combat even difficult situations.

2. *Wealth and material accumulation do not make anyone happy.* Success can mean many things to different people, but living a successful and peaceful life has little to do with how wealthy you are. The best car, the biggest house, and other material items may provide happy hours or days, but only temporarily. The things that truly bring peace are the kind people around you and the beauty the world provides naturally. You don't need much more than sharing kindness with others, enjoying an effort to be kind. Appreciate loving friends that are available in your present life. Safeguard your values and respect the world around you.

3. *No one can always be right.* Wasting time trying to prove you are right weakens your connections with others, and even prevents you from developing as a normal person. Respecting the beliefs of other cultures and learning new things can change your perspective. Even if you don't agree with a person, there is peace in taking a deep breath and accepting that you and this other person hold different views on certain aspects of life. It's okay if you agree to disagree. Your soul provides peace when you reduce the conflict based on your need to be right.

4. *No one has all the answers.* No human being has the correct answer to every question in life. Some people know what their passion is immediately.

Finding Peace

However, many of us struggle to discover which achievement will satisfy our life. Some of us focus our efforts to attain a goal. In the process we feel fulfilled. Years later, we realize that attaining our goal was not as important. There is nothing wrong with not finding the answer to what we really want in our life. Maturity comes with age and experience. One morning you may wake up fully aware that you have the right answer for a question you had yesterday. It is a moment of enthusiasm that has surfaced from within you. And, being excited, you say, *Aha, I know what I need to do and I'm willing to work for it.*

5. *Your real self is a blessing.* Many of us have dreams that require risk, doing things that feel scary. It's normal to doubt yourself and wonder if you will succeed or if you are making a mistake. You can go to college and get that degree. You can learn the skills necessary to become talented in that specific area. With the right amount of determination and persistence, you can complete that triathlon. Remember that the tool kit is within you. Just give yourself a chance. You can achieve peace by realizing that everything you need is in you. You are enough.

6. *Avoid those who are envious or negative.* Unfortunately, all of us will encounter people who may hurt us on various levels. An old friend might betray you. A romantic date might prove to be insensitive and disrespectful. The person you have valued as a dear friend suddenly disrespects and devalues you, despite all the efforts you have made to keep

the friendship alive. Trying to change these people or yourself is not going to gain their friendship. Simply, do what you can to make peace with people with whom you have an issue. If you have hurt someone, unintentionally or not, then apologize. Be kind and loving. It is time to step away and give that person space for healing. Depending on the extent of the pain caused, the person hurt or both of you may need time to let go of past pain and learn to forgive. Peace can thrive in your heart when you surround yourself with caring people who treat you with respect and kindness.

7. *Clutter absorbs energy.* Create a personal space where you relax and experience peace. You might have your own idea of what clean and tidy looks like. Create a personal space that makes you feel good every day—a place where you feel comfortable. When you come home and feel overwhelmed by the mess you encounter or find yourself hoarding items that are no longer relevant to your life, it may be time to do some serious decluttering. Holding on to unnecessary items absorb your energy. At best, give them away or get rid of them.

8. *You are not alone.* When experiencing difficult problems, you may feel alone, like nobody can understand the despair that you are going through. Trust that there are others who share a similar journey and are struggling and persevering with challenges just like you. On your journey, you may even meet some of these people who will help open your heart to the strength and love within you.

Finding Peace

9. *A peaceful life is not totally free of pain.* Pain is a healthy part of being alive. There will be times when you struggle to face recurring problems at home or at work, or when things you love are suddenly taken from you. Relocating to a new city can be terrifying and painful at first. Pursuing a new career can be downright scary. Stepping out of your comfort zone can be intimidating. While life grants us an abundance of joy and happiness, it also offers trials and pain along the way. Accept the good and tough parts of life. You can still live a peaceful life knowing that when you get through the struggles you will be stronger.

10. *The journey of life counts, not the destination.* Many of us chase goals and wonder why we feel discontent with life. Filling your schedule with goals and ambitions may feel great at the time, but it leads to a cycle of believing that achieving a goal will lead to peace and happiness. It is most important to create a life that honors and respects your values. For instance, you will feel much happier creating a life where you prioritize your health. Goals are a terrific way to set milestones and measure how far you have come, but achieving a goal does not lead to peace. The journey is what creates a peaceful life.

7

THE PURSUIT OF PEACE

This is my wish for you: peace of mind, prosperity through the year, joy that multiplies, health for you and yours, fun around every corner, energy to chase your dreams, contentment to fill your daily life.

—D. M. Dellinger

We all need peace. Tired and exhausted after a day's work, pressured by tasks, family responsibilities, and social obligations, we feel stressed out. What keeps us from having peace and harmony in our life? Possibly fear, insecurity, and worry? Whenever we feel physically or emotionally tired, when we sense that our security is threatened, we become angry, defensive, and anxious. This is true for individuals, spouses, groups, and communities.

Once we arrive safely in our home, like an airplane reaching its base, we feel relief. The familiarity of our environment offers peace. But what if we bring home difficult issues that we faced outside our home, difficulties that have eventuated during the day?

CARING FOR THE SOUL

Many people seeking solutions to their conflicts turn to professional help. Others might call a close friend to vent, hoping to find support. Inner peace is not just for those who dedicate their lives to prayer or spirituality. Inner peace is attainable regardless of our lifestyle or occupation. Inner peace can be found as we learn to mindfully view the reality of who we really are and how we perceive the reality of the world around us.

If we are serious about caring for our soul, we need to have peace of mind. Without it, our spiritual life and our soul suffer, and we may even experience physical symptoms. We are all subjects to our present condition—the noise of modern life that makes it hard to focus. Radios drone in our houses, cars, at work, and even follow us into the grocery store, stalking us down the aisles. Television invades our living room with other people's lives and dramas, artificial words and images, leaving little space for our thoughts. Computers, texting, and smartphones absorb moments that we might otherwise use to enjoy some peace.

Why is inner peace important? The pursuit of inner peace is more important and vital than the search for happiness or success. Happiness is a temporary experience; like a fleeting emotion, it only lasts for a while. Success can be taken from us just as easily as it can be gained. But true inner peace, once attained and maintained, is lasting.

Inner peace is a state of emotional and mental peace, without disturbing thoughts, that recognizes our control over our moods and reactions. As believers, to attain this peace we must overcome our negative thoughts and fears, learn to accept who we really are in the eyes of God, cultivate our faith, trust in the presence of Jesus Christ, and apply his teachings. Peace must be a balanced effort of mind, heart, and spirit, a right attitude that does not hurt anyone but benefits us and possibly others.

When Jesus spoke of peace, he meant peace as an inner condition, not attained without intense effort. "Glory to God in the highest heaven, and on earth peace among those whom he favors" (Luke 2:14). To attain the peace that Christ promised, we must reconcile ourselves with others and harmonize our lives with our surroundings. "Peace I leave with you; my peace I give to you. I do not give to you as the world gives. Do not let your hearts be troubled, and do not let them be afraid" (John 14:27). We need to have an active part in the blessing of peace. We cannot simply be quiet recipients, expecting others to make peace with us or bring peace to our lives. If we want to cherish the peace that Christ promises, we need to develop an attitude of reconciliation between self and others, making amends where there is conflict that we may restore peace. Those who help establish God's peace—whether providing care to those in need, helping neighbors, restoring unity within their family, or helping to reconcile a divorcing couple—are recognized as assisting in Christ's mission in our world.

While God may not have physical hands to reach out and embrace those who need comfort, we become the instruments to show his love. "By this everyone will know that you are my disciples, if you have love for one another" (John 13:35). And St. Paul states, "For he is our peace; in his flesh he has made both groups into one and has broken down the dividing wall, that is, the hostility between us" (Eph 2:14). We cannot find peace if we harbor anger and hostile feelings.

The peace that Christ offers surpasses our human understanding, and it comes to us as we attune our life with God's will. God will give this peace to us when we work with all our strength and use our gifts to do something good and beneficial for others. Developing a sense of inner peace means that we are willing to see our little hypocrisies and large illusions and learn to be more honest with ourselves and with others. We regain peace when we see with clarity the true nature of things. An apple is an apple. It cannot be an orange, nor can an orange become an apple. Our friend, our spouse, our parents, siblings, or our boss—each one is who he or she is. None can be like us because each character is individual and unique. We cannot conform to another's lifestyle and be at peace.

Regarding a joyful and peaceful spirit, St. Paul writes,

> Rejoice in the Lord always; again I will say, Rejoice. Let your gentleness be known to everyone. The Lord is near. Do not worry about anything, but in everything by prayer and supplication with thanksgiving let your requests be made known to God. And the peace of God, which surpasses all understanding, will guard your hearts and your minds in Christ Jesus.
>
> Finally, beloved, whatever is true, whatever is honorable, whatever is just, whatever is pure, whatever is pleasing, whatever is commendable, if there is any excellence and if there is anything worthy of praise, think about these things. Keep on doing the things that you have learned and received and heard and seen in me, and the God of peace will be with you. (Phil 4:4–9)

Peace can only come when people are receptive to it and become peacemakers themselves.

When we attain inner peace, we can cope, in a healthy way, with any event or situation happening around us. Inner peace does not take away or eliminate our anxieties or fears, rather it allows us to cope with those anxieties and fears, through which we learn and move toward a healthier life. Finding and living with inner peace is possible. Once you can believe this you too can work toward gaining inner peace.

FOR FURTHER CONSIDERATION

The following are a few reasons outlining the importance of inner peace. In no way is this list exhaustive, but rather one to build on:

✦ Inner peace improves our ability to focus our mind. In today's world there are many distractions that cause anxiety and worry. The anxiety and worry that we might experience is not productive and causes us to lose focus on ourselves and our families. Inner peace promotes proper coping methods so that we can act while maintaining our focus on what is truly important.

✦ It helps us to show patience and tolerance. If you have any dealings with social media, you are fully aware of the lack of tolerance and patience in people these days. Inner peace allows us to be patient and tolerant of the views of others without the need for angry reactions or negative responses. Inner peace promotes better understanding of the situation and solutions to the problems we face.

✦ It allows us to sleep better. Many of us do not get the proper amount of sleep because our bodies or our minds are overworked. Inner peace helps us to cope with stress and anxiety, and allows our minds not only to focus but to slow down and gain adequate rest.

✦ It brings happiness. Happiness is but a fleeting emotion and does not happen easily these days. Inner peace allows us to experience our happy moments more deeply. As we practice mindful living and a sense of inner peace, those moments of happiness feel greater and seem to last longer.

✦ It improves our relationships. How we feel about ourselves is how we perceive the world around us. That perception of the world guides our responses and actions. Inner peace elevates my self-image, and therefore the world seems better and brighter and leads to more positive reactions and actions on my part. The more positive my relationships, the more positivity I receive from others.

8

CARING FOR YOUR SOUL

Soul-caring is a life-time effort, intuition, inspiration, skill and courage. Most of us yearn excessively for entertainment, control, power, intimacy, sexual fulfillment, and material things. We think we can somehow find these things but whatever we find, does it satisfy the soul?

—St. Thomas More

If you want to take care of the most important part of yourself, your soul, prepare your heart not for food, not for drink, not for rest, but for a battle against adverse forces, so that you may endure all temptations, trouble, and sorrow. Prepare for severities, spiritual struggles, and for many trials and afflictions. We must consider all adversities, even passions that war against us, causing other unnecessary distractions. You can only conquer a passion when you no longer consider it as part of you. This is very important.

When we are experiencing pain, the caregiver is a very important part of the recovery process. Attentive doctors,

CARING FOR THE SOUL

nurses, therapists, a loving spouse, parents, children, and friends comfort us when we are ill and speed our recovery process. There are times when, no matter how independent we may be, we must entrust others with our care. We must surrender to them, for they assist us in the healing process.

Basically, the Lord Jesus is the ultimate caregiver. When we surrender ourselves to the Lord, we give up whatever is causing our pain and turn everything over to him. "Cast your burden on the Lord, and he will sustain you; he will never permit the righteous to be moved" (Ps 55:22). Through faith and trust in the Lord, we make ourselves eligible to be partakers of the salvation offered by Jesus Christ so that, one day, we may return and be welcomed to live with him.

Taking care of your soul, the immortal part of you, implies an ongoing awareness as you interact with the world around you in thought, word, or action. Make each encounter—be it with your spouse, mate, child, sibling, friend, boss, colleague at work, and so forth—a spiritual one. Instead of antagonizing those whose personality or opinion is different from yours, show them acceptance, compassion, respect.

What is the care food for our soul? Besides regular prayer, it is reading, reflecting, and meditating on the Scriptures. Here again, ponder the Word of God and what it means to you as you apply it to your life. When we pray, or speak to God, we are connected and encouraged by our soul. To pray for any length of time, we must have at least a small desire to connect with our Creator. A good time to pray is after our inner self, our soul, has been nourished by meditation on the Word of God. It is then that we find our Lord speaking to us, comforting us, encouraging us, instructing us, accepting us, and directing us. When we allow a few minutes for meditation, it

Caring for Your Soul

can be much easier to stay focused. In applying this practice, myself, God has given me courage and strength to go through greater challenges than I had ever thought possible.

Many people, whose souls are troubled, understandably feel anxious or depressed and resort to psychiatry, or psychotherapy, or to other methods of healing. Truly, each of these disciplines has importance, and in time of need, each makes a significant contribution toward a healthier life. Each method can relieve people from anxiety, depression, emotional pain, and possibly from negative moods and emotions; each can uncover bad life choices, human mistakes, and unhealthy habits or bad programming, and, without criticism or judgment, provide some of the best lessons in life.

Most people that have come to me for therapy seek solutions to their problems and direction in life. They tell me how unhappy they are, facing conflicts, anger, depressing feelings. While we cannot control life's challenges, we can, at least, take charge of our own personal life. As a therapist, I aim to instill self-confidence in my clients, a capacity to look toward each day with some courage, optimism, positive thoughts, patience, persistence, and excitement.

Most of my clients, for one reason or another, tell me they are not happy. Only recently, a young couple who sought my help surprised me. "It's not that we are unhappy, but we feel that something is missing in our life." I had met Bob and Debby at church and at social events sponsored by our community. One Sunday after church services, we happened to sit at the same table for coffee and we all introduced ourselves. They have been married more than three years and have a little boy named Andy. Both appeared to be happy with their respective jobs.

When I mentioned that I was in practice of psychotherapy and marriage therapy, Debby unexpectedly asked, "Can Bob and I come and see you sometime?"

"Of course, you can," I said.

"Not that we are unhappy with our life, but Debby and I have some questions."

"I'll be honored when I'm able to answer even some of your questions," I said.

Friday of the following week, Bob and Debby came to my office after work. Jovially and with smiles, they sat close to each other across my desk. By appearance, they seemed to be a good looking and loving couple.

"What's the feeling you are experiencing right now?" I asked.

"I feel a bit anxious," Bob said.

"And you, Debby?"

"I feel restless and frustrated," Debby said.

"I feel the same way," Bob added, with anxiety evident in his eyes.

"Could either of you tell me what's going on in your life?"

"Debby is good at describing feelings. She can be the spokesperson," Bob said and pulled back comfortably in his seat.

Debby looked at him with a guarded smile and said, "Okay Bobby, I'll tell the doctor why we are here."

Bob and I nodded with silent approval.

Debby eagerly began. "It's not that we are unhappy. Our lives are good. We care for and love each other, but they seem too insignificant." Bob, hearing his wife's tone, shook his head in agreement, relieved as she continued: "We want to do something more important and significant than what we have both been doing since we began our married life. We want to do something legendary that could be appreciated and written about. The town where we live, the different jobs we both have, our friends, our relationship with each other, the church that we attend—somehow things do not seem enough. It is our hope that our loving son, Andy, will have a more rewarding life than we have had this far."

For the first time in many years of doing marriage therapy, I found myself unable to respond to Debby's lack of fulfillment or undefined expectations. Could I tell Debby and Bob that most people feel disappointed with their life because, to a certain degree, we are limited, inadequate, blemished, dull human beings, and our soul, the spiritual part of our being, is neglected and thirsts for care and attention? No matter how rich and attractive our personalities, no matter how successful and materially wealthy we have become, none of us can indefinitely generate novelty and psychological pleasure in life. We cannot be excited all the time. But as we focus, being grateful for what we have and nurturing our inner self, our souls will regain peace and joy that can be lasting.

As our first session ended, I said, "If you wish to come back for marital counseling, I would like to see you one at a time. Either one of you can come first, and after I get to know each of you better, I can see you together."

They agreed. Then Debby asked, "Aren't you going to give us any homework today?"

"No homework, but I'm tempted to tell you a Greek poem that offers a lasting lesson:

An old man, known as blind George
grasped his cane in one hand and in the other, he
held his child.

*One day, he set out on a long journey to find the
   secret of joy.
In the squares of towns he came to,
elders shared the shade of a plane tree,
discussing events of long ago.*

*The rich and famous set him a place at their tables,
but there was no joy in their faces.
Joy was always ahead of pursuit.
George, the sightless man, needed vision;
the mystery eluded him still.
In his darkness, he tracked the unseen,
not a chance in his blind plight,
to gain sight but only once,
and find joy in his child.*

"Thanks Doc, that's a powerful poem," Bob said. "We need to be grateful for our little Andy." And Debby added, "Thanks for the poem. It can be our homework."

FOR FURTHER CONSIDERATION

✦ Most people have too much going on in their daily lives and not enough time to enjoy things that are important. Simplifying our life makes room for us to cherish and benefit from more important things. It also reduces stress and clutter, and that leads to a happier and more peaceful life. Each day of your life, each breath, and each heartbeat—all functions of your body—are God's gift to you. If you believe in God as the Creator of all things, vis-

Caring for Your Soul

ible and invisible, you may choose what is good for you and beneficial for your health and for your happiness.

✦ To be healthy and happy in your present life, you might consider doing something for the benefit of others. "Others" could be people with whom you associate: family members, coworkers, and individuals that you come across daily.

✦ In considering self-acceptance, appreciate what you have accomplished thus far. Do you enjoy your family and cherish the presence of your partner and children to the extent that you couldn't live without them?

✦ Life has its shadows: there is always the sense of not enough, the need to be in control, the inability to please everybody, the desire to compete and surpass all others.

✦ Perfectionism doesn't make you perfect. It makes you feel inadequate. You are not worthless because you cannot do it all. You are human. You can't escape that reality, nor can you expect to. Self-acceptance is the goal.

✦ During difficult times, faith and prayer pave the path that leads to God. In your own way, connect with him. In adversity, there is blessing. Allow God into your life as you contemplate Scripture: "When the cares of my heart are many, your consolations cheer my soul....But the Lord has become my stronghold, and my God the rock of my refuge." (Ps 94:19, 22)

✦ When your plans are impeded or fail, remember that "the Lord knows our thoughts" (Ps 94:11) and has other plans for you—a new direction, a new perspective. It may be hard for your mind to perceive the idea that God is totally aware of your needs. You may wish to see quick and easy results. But God's special plan can only be perceived by faith, which is an activity of the heart. This requires patience, persistence, and prayer.

9

THE QUEST FOR HAPPINESS

True happiness is...to enjoy the present, without anxious dependence upon the future.

—Lucius Annaeus Seneca

Happiness has been the human yearning from the beginning of time. God created a universe with unimaginable wisdom, beauty, and perfection. As a master artist, God adorned creation with spectacular forms and shapes. All creation, from a minute blade of grass, to shrubs, trees, flowers, and the stars, serve meaning and purpose and leave us in utter wonder.

We read in the Bible that after completing the inanimate world, God created Adam and Eve, the masterpiece of all creation. God created human beings with extra loving care and special intimacy, molding them out of earth—*Let us make humankind in our image and likeness*—and placed them in the garden of Eden, a wonderful paradise with an extraordinary abundance of beauty to provide happiness. We can sense God's infinite love. Like a caring father, God wanted all humans to be happy.

The path leading to happiness and success is different for everyone because each person is unique in their expectations, perceptions, and understanding of God's love. Because of this, each of us must find our own path and be aware of and clear about our expectations in life, or we will have a hard time receiving God's gracious gifts and recognizing his presence in our life. Unfortunately, our culture does a poor job teaching us how to find the path that leads closer to our Creator, where there is peace and happiness. Consequently, we are still searching for happiness.

While we are all searching for happiness, the approach to happiness is different for each individual. We may be endowed with the wisdom of Solomon and the resourcefulness and intelligence of Odysseus, yet still be unable to live a life of contentment. Many persons search for happiness in wealth and glory. They spend a lifetime, sacrificing their health and families, to become rich. We may admire them, assuming that they are happy, yet, we know well that the rich, famous, and successful have not necessarily found happiness.

Regardless of the money and material accumulations, these people are not content; they still want more. The idea of enough is nonexistent. In addition, some of them may be afraid and worry that something may go wrong and they could lose everything. What then happens to their wealth and glory?

We can hardly grasp God's inscrutable will and plan. Yet we know and believe that when humanity fails, God still loves creation. Throughout the Old Testament, we read of the prophets and wise men who God sent to restore the relationship with humanity. In time, God sent his only Son, Jesus, to bring us salvation—reconciliation, comfort, healing, forgiveness, love, peace—and life everlasting.

Consequently, when we fail and suffer, God pulls us out of our misery, forgiving us and restoring our life. God's love is unconditional. As John reminds us: "For God so loved the world that he gave his only Son, so that everyone who believes in him may not perish but may have eternal life" (John 3:16). In light of God's unconditional love, St. Peter offers advice in finding true happiness: "Above all, maintain constant love for one another, for love covers a multitude of sins. Be hospitable to one another without complaining. Like good stewards of the manifold grace of God, serve one another with whatever gift each of you has received" (1 Pet 4:8–10).

Happiness or unhappiness is the result of our evaluation of a given situation. If we judge a situation as bad, we tend to feel uncomfortable and unhappy; if we judge a situation as good, we feel positive and happy. The experience of happiness is often a general term we use to say that we feel good—physically, mentally, emotionally. Most of us use different terms to describe what feels good. For someone it might be excitement, passion, exhilaration, fulfillment, freedom, feeling fully alive with inspiration and joy; for another it might be peacefulness, contentment, hope, satisfaction, and comfort.

Regardless, our natural state of being is to be happy. In fact, when you remove all the uncomfortable emotions, we are left with happiness. Therefore, it is possible to define happiness by what it is not. Happiness is when you're *not* feeling self-doubt, depressed, hateful, fearful, worried, unsatisfied, bored, grieved, shamed, guilty, discontent, anxious, annoyed, angry, irritated, stressed, frustrated, upset, sad, envious, or jealous. Whew! That's a lengthy list! True happiness is to be free from anxieties and physical pain; to understand and do our duty to God and our fellow human beings; and to enjoy the present without anxious dependence on the future.

FOR FURTHER CONSIDERATION

✦ The quest for happiness involves taking personal responsibility. Instead of blaming others for your unhappiness, figure out ways in which you can be happy despite *external* circumstances and the *negative* behavior of others.

✦ It is possible to be happy no matter what the external circumstance. Your mind can make a heaven of hell or a hell of heaven. A person who has taken personal responsibility recognizes an all-important truth about happiness: it depends much more on your attitude than it does on external circumstances.

✦ Ask yourself whether you can be happy in the ordinary circumstances in which you find yourself daily. Can you, for example, entertain the possibility of being happy even though it's raining outside? Can you be happy if a meeting with your employer did not go as well as you would have liked?

✦ Consider your emotional responses to events as a muscle. Just as your biceps become stronger only when you exercise them, your ability to control your emotional response gains strength only when you take on challenges that are commensurate with your current ability.

✦ Sometimes you may find yourself unable to maintain a positive attitude due to a negative event. This just means

The Quest for Happiness

that you don't, at present, possess sufficient control over your mind to feel happy regardless of the circumstances. You may ultimately desire to be like Jesus Christ, who remained focused on his relationship with God, his Father, in these times of struggle—but this takes time and prayer.

10

THE QUEST FOR JOY

*This is the day that the LORD has made;
let us rejoice and be glad in it.*

—Psalm 118:24

In our previous chapter, the emphasis was on happiness. Every normal human being wishes to be happy and our culture tirelessly provides means and ways to make people happy. Naturally, because each person is unique in his or her expectations and perceptions are different, the question is, What could possibly make them happy? Even if they have a period of happiness, it does not seem to last long, and their search continues.

What this chapter proposes is to start looking for God's gift of joy that has a lasting value. God's gift of joy is a positive inner feeling, a transcendent contentment. It is a spiritual force induced within each person by the Creator. Next to genuine love, joy may be the deepest creative power in human nature. Rooted in the riches of our spiritual nature, it precipitates a healthier response to life, a more loving encounter with one another, and a beneficial interaction with the world around us. It is an evidence of appreciation of life as a blessing, a gift, and a value. A joyful heart *knows* the mystery of life.

Webster's dictionary defines *joy* as "the emotion evoked by well-being, success, or good fortune, or by the prospect of possessing what one desires." We can think of joy as the emotion expressed when a person is in a state of happiness. When we are grateful and content for whatever is available to us—physical health, a good job, family, freedom, friends—we express our satisfaction through joyful speech, warmth, laughter, and other joy-filled responses. To experience joy implies that we interact with others with genuine interest and a good disposition, revealing a positive and kind attitude. Love and friendship, leisure time, and opportunities to be creative and to serve society are healthy resources of joy.

In the presence of caring people, loving parents, and close relatives and friends—where we feel accepted and loved—we experience that special feeling. Reading a good book, attending a meaningful play or movie, visiting another country, sitting by the ocean and observing the waves, or walking through the woods and breathing the fragrance of the trees—each experience can create a basis for inner exuberance. As we observe and respond to nature's colors: the sunrise, sunset, sky, mountains, trees, and flowers, our spirit rises and we sense a new energy fueling that unique feeling of exhilaration. We can then appreciate the psalmist's ecstasy, when he said, "O Lord, how manifold are your works! In wisdom you have made them all" (Ps 104:24).

It is interesting that the word *joy* appears 165 times in the Bible. It denotes that God created us for joy and love, yet our world is inundated by many families and individuals who

The Quest for Joy

have no joy in their lives. In Psalm 16:11, the author speaks of God, "You show me the path of life. In your presence there is fullness of joy." There is a reassurance in the Holy Scriptures that calls on people to have joy and to celebrate life. God wants his people to have that empowering emotion, which energizes and makes them creative and sensitive to the needs of others. The good news is that we are able and can do something to relieve suffering and bring a ray of hope to our afflicted brothers and sisters. As we reach out a helping hand, we will sense an inner feeling of joy. Our minimal help may appear a drop in the ocean, but it is the many drops that make the ocean.

Joy can be fragile if it is only externally induced. Occasionally grief, being a strong emotion, may overshadow our joy. Yet joy continues to be an inner condition, and it is essential to our existence. Sometimes, when a dark cloud of displeasure and misery hovers over us, we can turn to our Lord Jesus and accept his loving and unconditional invitation—"Come to me, all you that are weary and are carrying heavy burdens, and I will give you rest" (Matt 11:28). In John's Gospel, we read, "I came that they may have life, and have it abundantly" (10:10). In John 15:11, he says, "I have said these things to you so that my joy may be in you, and that your joy may be complete." During his troublesome and dark days, remorsefully King David implored God, "Restore to me the joy of your salvation" (Ps 51:12). He wanted relief from his painful past.

As we accept the fact that a part of us is divine, and believe that God is always present in our lives and his plan is to restore the joy he wants us to have, we will begin to experience the joy of his continuing care, forgiveness, and love. In his eyes, we are the stars of the earth. The stars of the sky shine only at night, but he gives us the light of his teachings to shine during the day by our positive thoughts, good feelings, healthy attitudes, and works of charity. The fruit of the Holy Spirit—love, joy, patience, kindness, generosity, faithfulness, gentleness, self-control—will be our reward and lasting treasure.

Joy fortifies family ties, relationships between spouses, parent and child, teacher and student, leader and follower, lover and loved. Joyous states of mind strengthen the individual and the bonds among members of a group. The spirit of joy encourages participation in activities that benefit higher goals. The Ancient Greeks, who understood the mysterious power of unseen things and pursued *to ev zein* (joyous living), bequeathed to us one of the most beautiful words in our language—the word *enthusiasmos* (enthusiasm; *en-theos-ousia*)—implying God's essence within. That reality is confirmed by St. Paul, who says, "I pray that, according to the riches of his glory, he may grant that you may be strengthened in your inner being with power through his Spirit, and that Christ may dwell in your hearts through faith" (Eph 3:16–17). The joy of a human being is to have God within, which implies that we feel good about who we are as children of God and have a reasonably healthy relationship with our Creator.

Being an inner feeling, joy needs to be nurtured with good thoughts and protected from distorted perceptions. If we are going through a tough time, feeling moody or depressed (as periodically each of us does), a sense of joy is absent. Chances are that we are telling ourselves we are inherently inadequate or just plain "no good." The more we stay with negative thoughts, the more we become convinced that we are essentially worthless. As a result, we develop an attitude of

The Quest for Joy

passivity—*nobody cares about me, why should I care about anybody or anything*—and we become paralyzed, unable to move and participate in the normal flow of life. If we continue to feel that way, eventually we will experience an emotional reaction—hopelessness, despair, rage, even self-hatred. In the chaos of negative emotional and hostile reactions, we see ourselves as deprived, defective, deserted, and defeated, with no ray of hope, no joy. St. Paul provides comfort as he says, "Rejoice in hope, be patient in suffering, persevere in prayer. Contribute to the needs of the saints; extend hospitality to strangers" (Rom 12:12–13).

It is strange that our human nature, while so richly endowed with nerves of anguish and so splendidly organized for pain and sorrow, is but poorly equipped for joy. A sense of ineffable joy, attainable at will and equal in intensity and duration, could go far to equalize any adverse situation that we may encounter. An effective way to emerge from the dark state of self-defeat and worthlessness that many of us go through is to visualize the possibility of a better life, which every human being is entitled to have. Initially, we try to identify and accept the reality of life as it is, including the ongoing physical changes. We become more aware of the physical, emotional, and mental changes—the thoughts, feelings, and behavior that we experience—as we mature. God did not create worthless human beings. He created us for joy and happiness. God loves us. "Who will separate us from the love of Christ? Will hardship, or distress, or persecution, or famine, or nakedness, or peril, or sword?...Nor anything else in all creation, will be able to separate us from the love of God in Christ Jesus our Lord" (Rom 8:35, 39). And that is the essence—that is the secret of joy—to feel loved and accepted unconditionally. He made that known to us, when out of unconditional love he became man, accepted and related with every aspect of our human nature. Christ, fully human and fully divine, lived among his people. He fed the hungry, healed the sick, forgave the sinners, resurrected the dead, pointed the way to real joy and peace through his teachings, and promised life everlasting. As we emulate his life and interact with other people with love, compassion, gentleness, goodness, and generosity, our life can be one of contentment.

Spring is the time of year that we leave behind the dreary cold days of winter months and we enjoy warmer weather and longer days. As we notice flowers, plants, and trees in flush, coming back to life again, our body, mind, and spirit feel refreshed and revitalized. At this time the Christian churches celebrate Easter, the resurrection of Christ. In a variety of customs and traditions, people attempt to give their life color and joy—Easter bunnies, egg hunts, chocolates, and special dinners.

The late Joseph Campbell, a renowned mythologist, left us with an excellent suggestion, if we can only practice it: "Follow your bliss." It does not mean doing whatever you want to, regardless of the cost to others; it does not mean doing whatever seems to feel good at the moment; it does not mean merely pursuing fleeting pleasures and sensations. Bliss is a taste of our spiritual nature, being in touch with the divine part of humanness, walking the path of life that leads to God. Instead of whining and whimpering over things we cannot change, we bank on an attitude of gratitude that a caring God is ever present.

To follow our bliss is therefore to do what expresses and opens us to our true nature and its source, our soul. For some this might be an involvement with a church related activity or a daily time out for prayer. It could be a visit to their place

The Quest for Joy

of birth, or being in an intimate dialogue with a loved one, or observing the growth of a child, or painting a picture, or planting a garden, or writing a book. For others, to follow their bliss may be to enjoy travel or to study the grandeur of nature. Still others may find joy engaging in charity work, helping the poor or the sick, and doing God's work.

Pleasure-seeking, which mass media encourages, gives transitory joy but inevitably precipitates disappointment. As we realize the limitations of physical delights, pleasant as they may be, we appreciate the delights of the spirit within, which is our birthright. The secret of joy lies in discovering who in the world we are and making the effort to accept the real self. We can never attain contentment until we learn to be true to ourselves and find the courage to be who we really are. *Being who we really are* and accepting *who we really are* lay the foundation of joyful living. Yes, we are God's sons and daughters, each one unique and different. If we try to be or imitate someone, we're not real; we may impress other people for a brief moment, but we will feel insecure and uncomfortable. But when we are willing to be authentic, to be genuine people, to be who we really are, we will experience joyful life. When our conscience is clear and we feel comfortable interacting with other people, we experience a lasting contentment. A good conscience is able to bear much, and it is not intimidated in adversities. A guilty conscience is always fearful and restless.

There is a risk when we begin to display our authentic self and *live out* who we really are. We may have to face some loss. We may permanently, yet unintentionally, offend or lose an intimate friend, cause a parent or a sibling or a relative to keep a distance from us, or put our job in jeopardy. But when we become authentic, we set ourselves up for the deepest kind of enduring joy. We discover the peace that accompanies a set of free and effective choices—the feeling of fulfillment and inner joy—realizing that we are under God's grace, completely capable of standing by our best attitude.

When we break free from the addiction of trying to please everybody so they can love us, we may be rediscovering the real world, because most people have their own interests. All our contacts are different, and it is unrealistic to be accepted, approved, and loved by every person that crosses our path. What seems to work is an effort to stand tall in the middle of life, strong in our convictions, responsible decision-makers, and comfortable with our strengths and weaknesses. We have a choice to apply our strengths and reduce our weakness to a minimum. As a result of this sort of authenticity, *being true to ourselves*, our heart will inevitably be filled with a steady and lasting joy.

FOR FURTHER CONSIDERATION

✦ A good way to develop a joyful attitude is to refine our thoughts and remove anger, judgment, jealousy, and any other negative notions that can burden the mind. With a clear mind we can work patiently on difficult problems and seek realistic solutions. We can take responsible action to put our life in order. Regardless of our external conditions, there is room in our heart for hope, as we begin to think and act joyfully.

✦ "Pretend that you are happy for a week" is a practical way that I suggest to certain of my clients who tend to wallow in despair. It seems to work with many people: *simply to pretend that they are happy*. I ask then to leave aside angry feelings, negative thoughts, and complaints, and try for a whole week to think, talk, and act as if your heart was bursting with joy. When they come back a week later, I sense the difference. Their attitude is more positive. Then, I ask them to continue the exercise for a second and third week.

✦ Are areas of dissatisfaction insurmountable, beyond our control, or could we transcend them? Whenever we are in a good mood, we need to observe how well we interact with other people, friends, relatives, or associates. A bad attitude will find wrongs with everything and everybody, even with the sun. A good attitude can be a reasonable goal for most of us because it is an internal condition. It is a state of mind. As we change our thoughts, our feelings change, and as a result, our behavior changes.

✦ External commodities, luxuries, and accumulations are not indispensable for that lasting feeling of joy. They provide happiness only for a while, and for a while they may pave the way for inner joy. Our turbulent times call for joy. On an inner level, joy means being true to one's self, genuinely honest, free from illusions and self-deception, ill-will, selfish bias, and prejudice. As joy emerges from the heart, it contributes to a better world because we are living our life in a caring manner.

11

THE FEAR OF DEATH

Death is a mystery. We know very little about it because we have not experienced it personally. Death is not always a tragic event, nor is it necessarily beautiful. The death of a young person or child is truly most painful for the parents and close relatives. Comforting words hardly bring any relief to the parents. Often, the best way to comfort and support a grieving person is with our presence. In the case of an elderly person, we might say, "Well, he or she lived a good long life. It was his or her time to go." Yet for the grieving family, regardless of how old the person is, the death leaves an emptiness in the family.

When death comes to a person whose last days are filled with illness, pain, and suffering, we often say, "It is a blessing that the person is no longer in pain." These words may sound trite, but when they come from the heart, they express sympathy.

The reality of death confronts us with emotional pain and the parts of our life that are still unfinished. To be able to accept death—as opposed to resigning ourselves to it—means that we have met the tasks and challenges of life and have reconciled our relationships.

The truth is that we cannot fathom the mystery of death. We do not even care to take a couple moments and think about it. We say to ourselves, *I know someday I will die.* But our thoughts seldom go any deeper. The fear seems instinctive, passed down to us through the generations. We have learned to tolerate the ever-present Grim Reaper; we know his scythe will eventually come our way, but for the present, we prefer not to confront him, not to tempt him, not to remind him of our existence.

We are all aware that our lives consist of stages and events for which we prepare. We prepare ourselves physically and emotionally for marriage, the birth of children, the upbringing and education of children, our middle years, our retirement, our everyday tasks. So we should also prepare ourselves for our final event, as fearful as we may be about it.

We must put our worldly affairs in good order. We may have known people who have departed and left behind confusion for others to sort out. If possible, one should express clearly to family members how one's possessions are to be distributed and one's wishes for the funeral and burial services. Often, family members do not want to listen or discuss such unpleasant issues, which is why preparing a will while our minds are sound and clear can be helpful. In addition to a will, we should take time to write a paragraph describing our fear. Getting started is the difficult part. Eventually, thoughts and feelings of fear will emerge from the depths of our consciousness.

The *first fear* concerns *the events leading up to our death*—failing powers, illness, prolonged pain, helplessness, and unfinished tasks. We each have our own assortment of

The Fear of Death

fears. Write down your own collection of fears so that you may look at them, examine them, and evaluate their importance.

The *second fear* concerns *the process of dying*—the ending of the body's activity. Anxieties over the body's sudden inability to function can be tremendously distressing. Anxiety can be difficult to appease. No sooner have you settled one anxiety than another emerges: *What if this should happen? What if that should happen?* It is like a series of predictions, none of which ever materializes. Dying has been described as a very natural process of passing away, like falling asleep. *Ekimithe en Kyrio*—"He or she has fallen asleep in the Lord"—is what some of the Greek Orthodox believers say to avoid mentioning the word *death*.

The *third fear* concerns *what happens after death*. Here, we have no scientific evidence to assist us. What we do have is our faith in a loving God who has brought us into life. As St. Paul says, "We do not want you to be uninformed, brothers and sisters, about those who have died, so that you may not grieve as others do who have no hope. For since we believe that Jesus died and rose again, even so, through Jesus, God will bring with him those who have died" (1 Thess 4:13–14).

Jesus in his human nature did not want to die, but when death came, he accepted it as part of giving his life to save us from our sins. By his dying and his resurrection, Christ robbed death of its power and delivered us from its terror. Faith in a God who plans to bring us back to himself through Jesus is cause for us to consider our lifestyle in this world. Strong faith, good works, acts of kindness and love, and efforts to forgive others and forgive ourselves will prepare us for God's kingdom. As our body returns to earth, in our new body we will find ourselves in the presence of our Lord Jesus Christ, where there will be unconditional joy, peace, and happiness.

Personally, I feel comforted in my conviction that the all-wise and loving God, who allowed me the privilege of visiting this planet for several years, will include me and each one of us in his divine plan. I have a favorite thought that comforts me daily and inspires my soul: My knowledge of the life to come is limited; the eyes of my soul are currently dim, but it is enough that Christ arose from the dead. And I pray that, when the time comes, I shall be with him forever.

"Well," you might say, "I also have faith, but I still experience fear when I think of death." That is normal. Most people feel the same. Consider two possible attitudes toward death: one is fear and inner turmoil, and the other is faith, acceptance, and peace. Most of us face death with fear. This fear has several ramifications. We fear death because we really do not know *how or when* it will happen to us. We have seen relatives and friends suffer for a long time before dying. Truly, such suffering causes fear.

Naturally, our thoughts of death generate sadness, as we realize that we lose all that we own and call our own, including our body, our hopes, and our dreams. As we leave this world and move on to an unknown destiny, we take nothing with us. We wonder about our own end: Are we going to be sick and suffer greatly? We fear the unknown: What happens after death? We fear leaving behind persons whom we have dearly loved all our life, and we consider how they are going to feel. We fear leaving behind material possessions that we worked very hard to obtain.

Fear has always been one of the most common attitudes toward death, despite society's attempts to avoid it. Facing death with acceptance and peace is a better attitude. Our body

The Fear of Death

is a temporary home. It is the masterpiece of God's creation. We take care of it with proper nourishment, we exercise to be healthy, and we try not to abuse it. Our true self—our soul—lives in this body and nourishes and cherishes the experience of our earthly life. We know that, as our body ages, our hair thins, our joints begin to ache, and we begin to feel weak, we are getting less young and need more sensitive care. At some point, the body becomes dysfunctional and, like any other part of nature, withers and fades away.

The thought of death is good and normal, for it prevents us from getting too wrapped up in this world and all the goods that it promises. Thinking of death keeps us close to the mark, for we do not know when we shall be called to the next life. It also makes us work harder, refining our thoughts and our life, helping others, and doing what God would like us to do. Knowing that our opportunities are strictly limited, not knowing the time of our death, we hasten to do some act of kindness because we may never have another such opportunity.

The more we accept this reality, the better we can let go of our body calmly and peacefully. Dying is a mysterious moment that each person experiences differently. Before the soul leaves the body, some people become aware of their life's actions, the good and the bad. Others have visions of deceased relatives or friends who are waiting for them. Still others see themselves traveling through a dark tunnel at the end of which is a bright light.

The acceptance of our mortality significantly reduces the fear of death. People who have accepted their own mortality can only hope that their close and dear ones can come to that position as well. Coping in different situations can also be handled on a more abstract plane; coming to terms with personal mortality makes it easier to deal with various situations in which the fundamental fears reside.

Acknowledging and accepting mortality means agreeing with the finality of our own lives. One reality to face is that life and living need to continue. Our loved ones who are left behind must continue in this life's journey. Their hearts may be heavy; their minds may be confused to see the person they loved dead. Nothing about grieving is inherently bad or wrong. Grief is a normal reaction when we lose someone we love.

As we become aware of our own mortality, can you consider the potential for new opportunities? Such an attitude may release mental and physical energy that can form the basis for new relationships and possibilities. For example, a dear friend lost her husband to a sudden heart attack and, four years later, lost her twenty-eight-year-old daughter in a car accident. After a long period of mourning and withdrawal from society, she mustered enough energy to face the outside world. Eventually, she found a man with whom she wanted to share the rest of her life. She moderately transcended her grief and new energy surfaced, producing the basis for a new relationship.

FOR FURTHER CONSIDERATION

✦ The soul forms the body, yet it is itself without a body. It is a spirit. It may be hard for anyone to see the beauty of the soul because of our engagement with the present world. Once the body ceases to function, the soul, being a spirit, separates from the body and returns to where it came from—back to God.

The Fear of Death

✦ As you embrace the potential that this life may not be the end but the beginning of another life, you may arrive at a gradual awareness and realization that life in this world cannot possibly be the end. It is but a new beginning, a new birth into a spiritual life.

✦ Observe yourself within, how some of your life's pursuits—goodness and beauty, justice and courage, forgiveness, friendship and loyalty, love and compassion—bring you lasting joy.

✦ Suppose you have only three months to live. It is truly a negative thought. Apart from the most loving person in your life, with whom would you like to be during this crucial period—a blood relative, a loving spouse, a son, a daughter, or a friend? You already know the answer.

✦ Persons who think about death during their middle or later years can feel very excited about the life that remains. Death cannot take away that excitement, because such people have accepted the reality of death; they enjoy life because they no longer fear life or death.

12

DEALING WITH GRIEF

I don't think of all the misery, but of all the beauty that remains.
— Helen Keller

In 1969, psychiatrist Elisabeth Kübler-Ross introduced what became known as the "five stages of grief." These stages were based on her studies of the feelings of patients facing terminal illness, but many people have generalized them to other types of negative life changes and losses, such as the death of a loved one or a breakup.

THE FIVE STAGES OF GRIEF

Denial: "This can't be happening to me."
Anger: "*Why* is this happening? Who is to blame?"
Bargaining: "Make this not happen, and in return I will ____."
Depression: "I'm too sad to do anything."
Acceptance: "I'm at peace with what happened."

If you are experiencing any of these emotions following a loss, it may help to know that your reaction is natural, and that you'll heal in time. However, not everyone who grieves goes through all these stages—and that's okay. Contrary to popular belief, *you do not have to go through each stage in order to heal*. In fact, some people resolve their grief without going through *any* of these stages. And if you do go through these stages of grief, you probably won't experience them in a neat, sequential order, so don't worry about what you "should" be feeling or which stage you're supposed to be in. Kübler-Ross herself never intended for these stages to be a rigid framework that applies to everyone who mourns. In her last book before her death in 2004, *On Grief and Grieving*, she said of the five stages of grief, "They were never meant to help tuck messy emotions into neat packages. They are responses to loss that many people have, but *there is not a typical response to loss, as there is no typical loss*. Our grieving is as individual as our lives."

In four decades of practicing marriage and family therapy, my personal experience in dealing with grief has been limited. To people who sought my counseling for a significant loss in their life, I made myself available with concern. Genuinely, I offered understanding for their pain and I tried to listen to their sadness with caring empathy. But being aware of my limitations, I referred them to a colleague, whose main practice is grief counseling.

So, how do we deal with or what do we say to a close friend or family member who has just experienced a loss? Many of us have no idea what to say or how to handle the situation. It is difficult to know what words to say to comfort someone grieving. It is natural to feel uncomfortable and unsure in this type of situation. We have so much fear of death or any kind of loss in our society that it is difficult to know how to handle our own emotional response, much less know how to support another person who is grieving. Nevertheless, there are simple and effective ways to help someone who is trying to cope with loss.

In time, after more experiences of dealing with grief surfaced, I arrived at the conclusion that silence is sometimes better than trying to fix the grieving person's problem. We may think helping someone in pain means helping them "get over" the problem, fast, but healing means learning to live with the loss, rather than getting over it completely. It is also important not to put a person's pain into perspective for him or her. For example, never compare a person's loss with someone else's or your own: "You think your mother's accident was bad. Last week, a very devout church member that I happened to know lost his wife and daughter in a car accident." Also avoid saying something like, "God doesn't give us any more than we can handle."

Our sympathetic presence in a grieving person's life is often the best way of offering comfort. And listening is better than talking and trying to impress someone with our wisdom and experience of suffering. We are human and pain is in all of us. It's okay if we don't know what to say when someone is in pain. People will believe you care if you just show up, even if you don't have much to say.

It is interesting that the one thing we are certain about in this life is that it will end, and yet, when that happens, we are never prepared. Emotionally we just don't seem to be well equipped to deal with such a loss—we either fall apart or head straight for denial. Grief is a normal, healthy response to loss, and we need to understand how to best deal with it in order to provide comfort to someone who is grieving.

Loss can come in many forms. As devastating as the death of a loved one can be, any life-altering experience can trigger a sense or feeling of loss and the stages of grief. Other losses include the loss of your health or the health of someone you care about, or the end of a relationship, such as a marriage or friendship. Healing from a loss involves coming to terms with the loss and the meaning of the loss in your life.

FOR FURTHER CONSIDERATION

✦ Showing up and being present where the loss has occurred is what is most needed. You may want to say something that might bring comfort, but words just don't seem to be enough, especially when people are dealing with intense grief.

✦ When you try to avoid clichés and common platitudes, it can be difficult to find the right words to convey what you want to say. Words can accomplish so much, but so does listening and being present. Along with being present, you can validate the feelings of someone who is grieving.

✦ Remember, you can't fix the pain of a grieving person. But you can provide comfort. You can do the best you can by offering consolation. When someone you care about is moderately coping with the loss of a loved one, you can gently say, "I'm truly sorry for your loss."

✦ Parents distressed over the sudden loss of their child (regardless of age) may be comforted by you keeping in contact. But make sure you do keep in contact. People in distress suffer more when they are left in the dark about when that contact will be made.

✦ We are all human and subject to unexpected loss. It's okay if we don't know what to say when someone is in pain. People will believe you care if you just show up, even if you don't have much to say or anything to bring.

13

PRUNING AND MATURING

For everything there is a season, and a time for every matter under heaven: a time to be born, and a time to die; a time to plant, and a time to pluck up what is planted.

—Ecclesiastes 3:1-2

Growing up on the Greek island of Lesvos, which is forested with olive and fig trees, I saw my father pruning branches mercilessly and cutting away sucker growths from the bottom of their trunk. I felt sad when I saw the fig tree become smaller in size.

"Dad, why did you cut away so many branches of the fig tree?" It was that beautiful and special tree that I used to climb to find the best, most delicious figs.

"Wait until spring when these trees will be rejuvenated, will have blossoms, and bear an abundance of fruit," my father replied, smiling proudly.

As an eight-year-old, I had a hard time believing that those fig and olive trees would ever survive after my father's radical pruning. But to my surprise, they did. Spring came and nature in full force proved that my father's words were on target. Both the olive and the fig trees brought us an abundance of fruit. My pruned fig tree gave us delicious figs through the entire summer.

As an eighty-eight-year-old man, I recalled the experience, realizing that pruning trees has become a metaphor for my life. Aging and ageless, I need to reflect and take heed of the benefits of pruning those aspects of my life that no longer serve a purpose. As I take an inventory each day, I focus on things of importance, letting go of what is unimportant.

Anytime I feel tired or exhausted from being overextended, I consider ways to simplify my life. In addition to pruning the external aspects of my life, and making it more manageable, I must also do some inner pruning.

When I feel overwhelmed, I search for the motive, fears, expectations, and habits that are causing me discomfort. In the quiet and gentle reflection, what is happening and the steps to correct it become evident.

Emotional availability to our significant others, family members, and friends relies directly on our ability to prune poor motivations, so we are not prey to unrealistic expectations—either ours or those around us. When we do this, the natural beauty of our life will spontaneously emerge and nurture others as well.

When we prune unrealistic expectations, the simple gifts that we have can be shared without much stress. We can reap rewards in unseen ways, no matter what the apparent results may be. But it is not easy to withstand the influence of a world so bent on overt accomplishments and public achievements. Still, when we set aside the need for ongoing successes and ceaseless praise, not only will we feel a sense of joy, but we will touch many others with that same joy.

When we do this inner pruning, we are more likely to be aware of the blossoms and the fruit we bring to those we encounter along the way. Knowing this helps us to step back and reassess when we feel overwhelmed by unrealistic expectations that others hold. This initial pruning relies on our ability to gain perspective and be clear about our goals, especially when we are exerting more and more effort but feeling less and less satisfied by what we are doing. Stepping back and reflecting on our motivations can make all the difference.

Most of us are good at seeing the problems that surface in our lives. We are also good at diagnosing what is causing them and planning what needs to be done about them. Yet, few of us take the next step and simply do what we can with a sense of joy and freedom. Instead, we focus on how small or inefficient our actions are. Once we are done with recognizing, diagnosing, planning, and acting, very few of us remember to let go. As spiritual people, who have done all that we can, we can let God take over.

FOR FURTHER CONSIDERATION

✦ Simplify. As we prune a tree, its growth improves to give more and better fruit or flower. Like pruning, as we simplify our life, we become better and more productive people. Simplifying one's life is a major step toward regaining energy and peace. By continually simplifying one's life, we create a harmony of inner peace and well-being.

✦ Set limits for daily tasks, things that need attention. I do it only once a day. Set time limits for small decisions and make them within seconds of thinking about them to avoid procrastination and overthinking. Set a limit for commitments, and don't be afraid to say no to reduce stress and produce better results.

✦ Avoid judging or criticizing. Acceptance of others, their looks, their behaviors, their beliefs, can transform anger and resentment into peace and tranquility. When you accept the reality of others, you stop feeding negative thoughts.

✦ Accepting what is doesn't mean giving up. It means that you put yourself in a better position to act if necessary. Because now you can see more clearly, you can focus your energy on what you want and act appropriately to change your situation.

✦ Practice forgiveness. Forgiveness is letting go of the past or letting go of the anger that you feel as you think of someone who has hurt your feelings. It is much easier to let go of things and to forgive what has happened. As humans, we let go and we allow God to do what he loves to do, to forgive.

14

YOU WILL NEVER DIE!

No one needs to fear death; the Savior's death freed us from it....Death, where is your sting? Hades, where is your victory? Christ is risen and you are overthrown. Christ is risen and demons have fallen. Christ is risen and angels rejoice. Christ is risen and not one dead remains in the tomb.

—St. John Chrysostom

As we approach the mystery of our soul's destiny after death, it is of great comfort to have faith and hope. St. John Chrysostom, a church father of the fourth century, convincingly reassures us, "No one needs to fear death. Christ is risen and not one dead remains in the tomb." As I visualize my death, especially the day of my funeral in the Orthodox Church—with priests, clouds of fragrant incense, eulogies, flowers, and chanting—melodic poetry and messages emerge from devout and warm hearts and rise straight to their own spiritual target, God.

The following is a small part of the funeral chant written by a monk of the East, John of Damascus (675–749):

Like a flower our human life withers, and like a dream
it vanishes. But when we hear The Call, we shall all rise to meet
the Lord. And shall ever be in his Glorious, Loving Presence.
What earthly sweetness remains unmixed with grief? What glory
remains immutable on earth? Once death comes, all human knowledge and
glory vanish like vapor. Lord God, among your saints rest the soul
of your servant who You have chosen today, in a place where life is
painless, peaceful and eternal.

This dramatic scene has no effect whatsoever on my well-groomed body lying soulless in the coffin. I feel no sadness or pain; yet in my soul is the full realization that this is the end of my earthly life. At this sad hour, I am surrounded by loving people, especially my family.

Pat, my loving wife, my children, grandchildren, and great grandchildren are sitting in the front pew with emotional pain shadowing their faces. Each one recollects sweet memories of the past. Periodically, they wipe their tears and possibly feel a tinge of anger, asking, *Why could he not have lived a little longer? I wish he was still with us.* Despite their profound grief, I envision every member of my family moving on with their individual lives; they must, because they are young and full of vitality, and I am happy for them. Life is for the living, and it is my joy to see them advancing in life, making good choices, living long, and cherishing God's blessings while on earth.

You Will Never Die!

During my life, any time the word *death* was mentioned, my wife's response was, "For you, death is not an option." Clearly, she genuinely loves me and does not want me to die. I do not want to die either, but do I have a choice? I know that death is the ultimate destiny of all living creatures. Accepting the fact that someday I will die, I decided to live the time that God has given me fully and with gratitude.

With practice, we can change our mindset from "Death is not an option" to *"Loving someone is to say that you will never die."* That might seem romantic, wishful thinking, but as Christians, we believe this is the truth of God's incarnation. If we take the incarnation seriously, that, out of his infinite love, God took on human flesh, then to love someone is to say to that person, "You will never die because, in this life and in the next, you will never be separated from God's family; by accepting God's love, you are closer and almost touching the body of Christ, just as those who were close to and touched Jesus physically during his time on earth. You will never die and there is nothing to fear after death because you are bound to Christ."

From time to time, we must examine our beliefs and feelings about death quietly and honestly. We can train ourselves to become less afraid of death and remove the erroneous perceptions of death as an enemy to be avoided. Initially, the thought of death can make us feel uncomfortable. Negative thoughts surface in our minds: What will our death be like? Will there be prolonged pain and suffering? Will we leave things unfinished? What about our loved ones, those we will leave behind? Such anxiety is normal.

Coming to terms with death requires quiet, positive thoughts. Death can be an important ally in our appreciation of life. We do not need to be morbidly worried or preoccupied with death. After all, it is better to be aware of our finitude as physical beings, realizing that our earthly existence is short and the time to love and be loveable is limited. The realization that, someday, we will inevitably die checks our attachments to the madness of our socially constructed existence. The thought of death can release our clings to material accumulation, social status, and superficial desires as sources of ultimate security. An awareness of death compels us to confront the reality of our existence.

Awareness that we will die awakens us from our social sleep to the reality of the human condition. Death is an unyielding partner in life—an inescapable certainty to push against as we sort out the significant from the trivial in our daily lives.

Our body is the vehicle that makes our journey on this planet possible. Compared to eternity, our journey is short, and life is like a dewdrop at the tip of a blade of grass that soon disappears with the rising sun.

Although the body is a temporary shelter—our home in this lifetime—it deserves respect and loving care. After death, the body will decompose and revert to its element—earth. To think of the body in this way is to realize the futility and transitory nature of all attachments. As an ancient hymn proclaims,

> *All mortal things are vanity*
> *since after death they are not.*
> *Wealth remaineth not,*
> *Glory goeth not with us.*
> *Death cometh suddenly,*
> *And all these things vanish utterly.*

While we are still alive, we have a choice to develop ourselves spiritually. It is only the spiritual development that we will carry into our next life.

We cannot hide from death. Its embrace will consume us entirely. Social positions, job titles, material possessions, sexual roles and images—all yield to death, the uncompromising friend that brings us back to the reality of life. This does not mean that we should abandon our material and social existence. Rather, by acknowledging our physical death, we are empowered to penetrate the social pretense, ostentation, and confusion that often obscures what is truly significant. In accepting the reality of death, we can more fully appreciate our gift of life.

LIVING LIFE TO THE FULLEST

Let us now consider how we can live so that death does not catch us unaware, "as a thief in the night." My wife, Pat, suggests that we should live our lives fully until we die. It is important to appreciate life, to live it in its fullness and maintain an attitude of gratitude.

Preparing for death does not need to be a morbid process. It should not distance, separate, or withdraw us from life, our spouse, children, and other family members. The very opposite is true. As Christians, what prepares us for death is a deeper, more intimate, and fuller entry into life. We get ready for death by beginning to live life as we should have been living it all along, by loving it. We prepare to die by pushing ourselves to love more, be appreciative, and be grateful to God for giving us another day. Along with the Psalmist, we can say, "This is the day that the Lord has made; let us rejoice and be glad in it" (Ps 118:24). Mindful that our earthly life comes to an end, death becomes an ever-widening entry into eternal life. Nobody dares think the best for us as much as God has already given us in his incarnation. If we really love someone, that person cannot die because Jesus Christ is loving him or her. If we forgive someone, that person is forgiven because Jesus Christ is forgiving him or her.

If our children, or any others we love, no longer go to church, our love for them and their love for us bind them solidly to the body of Jesus. They continue to touch the hem of the garment of Jesus so surely as did the woman in the gospel story who suffered with a hemorrhage.

We do not live daily with a direct and conscious appreciation of the world around us. Instead, we live almost completely immersed in a socially constructed reality that so fully absorbs our energy and attention that virtually no energy remains to experience the wonder of our existence. The tragedy of modern industrial cultures is the superficiality that we accept and, indeed, maintain as the common denominator in human affairs. We unconsciously trivialize the human experiment with shallow pursuits of money and social status that mask rather than celebrate the magnificence of the human being.

It is our belief in Christ, his teachings, and his presence that can enrich our life. God is not hidden and hard to contact; forgiveness, grace, and salvation are not the prerogatives of the lucky and the few; we don't have to save ourselves; we don't have to get our lives perfectly in order to be accepted and saved; we don't have to make amends for our sins; human flesh and this world are not obstacles, but part of the vehicle to heaven; we can help each other on the journey; love, truly human love is stronger than death; and to love someone is indeed to say, *You will never die!*

FOR FURTHER CONSIDERATION

✦ When we are affected emotionally by beauty, then our soul is alive and well. Basically, the word *passion* means "to be affected," and passion is the essential energy of the soul.

✦ Music can also nurture the soul. There is a reason that singing is universally used in worship. Emotionally, mentally, and physically singing evokes positive feelings that connect us with God. Singing is a means by which the spirit and the soul can interact to glorify God.

✦ Whenever the thought and feeling of connecting with our Creator becomes stronger, it is a movement made freely by our spirit. The spirit moves upward, expanding like the sound of a song into the space of our soul.

EPILOGUE

We are not human beings having a spiritual experience. We are spiritual beings having a human experience.

—Teilhard de Chardin

After reading the thoughts and ideas recorded in this book, you may wonder where these thoughts and ideas came from. If they were the product of the mind, would not your mind also have known these thoughts and ideas? So, why did I bother to write this book? The most important relationship that we have in our adult lives is the relationship that we have with ourselves, our relationship with God, and with our soul. If our eyes are the windows of our soul, then our emotions, what we really feel, are the voice of our soul.

Because our soul speaks to us in soft voices and whispers, it often goes unheard. Our minds and our hearts being preoccupied with life's challenges get most of the attention. Our soul, our spiritual life, can unwittingly be neglected.

Since my ninetieth birthday, when I made a conscious choice to listen to my inner self, my soul's whisper, my life has completely changed. I needed to be still, focused, and attentive for long enough to be able to hear what my inner self, my soul, was communicating to me. After I authored twelve self-help books and two novels, I heard the gentle whisper of my soul saying, *What about me? You have fulfilled your passion for writing, helping people who needed guidance and support. Now you must feel like being rewarded. When will you find time to take care of me, your inner self, your soul?*

The challenge was evident! I needed to start caring for my soul. But where do I start? What are my soul's needs? *Could you use your passion for writing?* That "gentle whisper" echoed within me. Having listened to my soul's voice, I decided to write this book. Is it possible that you have bought and have read this book because you have heard *your soul's gentle voice*?

Today, I sat quietly and asked myself two questions: What does my soul want from me at this moment, and how and where do I start? Within seconds, the answer surfaced in my mind: *start with God's book*. I opened my Bible to the Book of Psalms. The psalms mirror a complex array of emotions and validate our deepest needs through poetry and songs. Like a great window into our souls, the psalms offer many insights. What is intriguing about the psalms is the relationship that develops between King David and his own soul. He holds real conversations with his soul.

For example, Psalm 42 begins with a poetic description of King David's soul longing for God's presence: "As a deer longs for flowing streams, so my soul longs for you, O God."

Then he asks, "Why are you cast down, O my soul, and why are you disquieted within me?" He encourages his soul to "hope in God; for I shall again praise him." He instructs, teaches, and urges it. He listens to its needs and desires and then points it toward God. King David is a good example in the art of caring for his soul. You and I cannot be King David,

Epilogue

but we can be motivated to emulate his experience by reading about how he feels about his soul.

Our challenge regarding how we relate to our soul needs an honest response. What is that inner relationship like? When was the last time we stopped our busy activities of fun, family, sports, cars, clothes, work, accomplishments, and a thousand other things and thought about our souls?

Five or more years ago, I did not give much attention to my soul. *I was too busy*. The awakening came later, when I started paying attention to my soul through prayer, charity, and truly caring for others. It was a time that I felt dry, confused, cracked, and abandoned, but I was too busy to stop and deal with my true feelings. As ironic as it sounds, staying busy with things for which I felt responsible became my primary way of avoiding my soul! Even the urgency and importance of our Christian mission to provide help for others was a convenient escape from the ever-increasing turmoil inside. Eventually, it was clear that I needed to stop the incessant pattern of doing things and start listening. I took a three-month break from all urgent activities and began exploring deeper needs, prayer, forgiveness, self-acceptance, and transformation. The sheer absence of activity and distractions was both strange and scary. I had to come to terms with everything I had been avoiding about myself, especially my relationship with God. I squirmed under the discipline of not doing things, and it felt weird. When I finally started listening to my inner voice, my life began the most incredibly joyous journey. It has taken me a long time to wake up and appreciate the pearls of wisdom my soul was offering me all those years.

Managing to work out regularly and having a healthy diet, I have become a disciplined, punctual, responsible person. People admire me. They often remark how peaceful and confident I seem. It's nice to have this image, but sometimes I don't feel the freedom to be human. I'm expected to be strong, peaceful, and confident all the time. But it's hard to maintain the image that some dear friends have of me and be true to myself. There are times that I feel tired and empty.

When we feel empty, alienated, or overwhelmed, we don't usually listen to what our soul is saying to us. It is panting, parched for a drink of God's love and life, but we've learned to drown our thirst for God with distractions such as television, shopping, music, a cold beer, the internet, texting, hobbies, parties—an incredibly busy schedule.

Take a few seconds today to be aware of how you shine in the world. Your true beauty dazzles the eyes and quickens the heart. When you live into that beauty, when you realize you own it, that's when the magic happens. Let go of your worries. You've been stressed. It's okay. Forgive yourself. Be kind to yourself. Today, you are not the person you were yesterday. Today, you can do better. Today, you will do better. You can't screw up this life—even if you try! Relax, knowing that you are an exquisite expression of divine love and grace. Nothing could mar this perfection. It is your truth to accept and allow in your life.

It's strange that we should ignore our soul this way. But because we believe in a loving and merciful God, it is never too late to start attending to our soul's needs. You might be on your way to work and find yourself running late—again. As you drive, your mind races from one thing to the next— being criticized by your boss for being late, remembering that it's your loved one's birthday and you forgot to buy a card. An unexpected noise in your car makes you slow down and think, *I need to take this car to a good mechanic*. The traffic light turns red. You stop and wait. In those few seconds of

Epilogue

silence, you begin to feel the emptiness in the air. Instinctively, you flip on the radio and comforting noise fills the hollow space for a little while.

Make this hour your first step toward caring for your soul. Close your eyes, take three deep breaths, and begin listening to your soul's whisper. Your soul is not judgmental. It will never put you down. Your soul is God's loving gift that only wishes the best for you. Your soul is a particle of God that abides in you and gives you life.

Hopefully, you have cherished the experience of reading this book as much as I have in writing it. This completion represents not an ending but a continuation of a journey. Caring for the soul is a daily lifelong journey and is worth making the most important focus in our life. Unlike any other aspect of ourselves, the more we care for the soul—nourish it, use it, even challenge it—the more accessible it becomes. Enjoy the benefits that your soul offers. The fact that this book has caught your attention says a great deal about your interest in the journey of enriching your relationship with your soul and your willingness to cultivate and cherish those aspects that are important in your life.

A Prayer for the End of the Day

*O Christ our Lord and God,
at all times and in every hour,
in heaven and on earth,
You are worshipped and glorified;
You are long-suffering, merciful, and compassionate;
You dear Lord,
love the just and show mercy upon the sinners;
You call everyone to salvation through the promise
of the blessings to come;
Lord, at this hour receive my humble prayer,
and direct my life according to Your commandments.
Sanctify my soul and body, refine my thoughts,
cleanse my mind;
deliver me from all distress and evil forces.
Encompass me with Your holy angels,
that guarded and guided by them,
I may attain the power of the faith,
and the knowledge of your divine presence.
For You are always blessed,
now and forever and unto the ages of ages. Amen.*